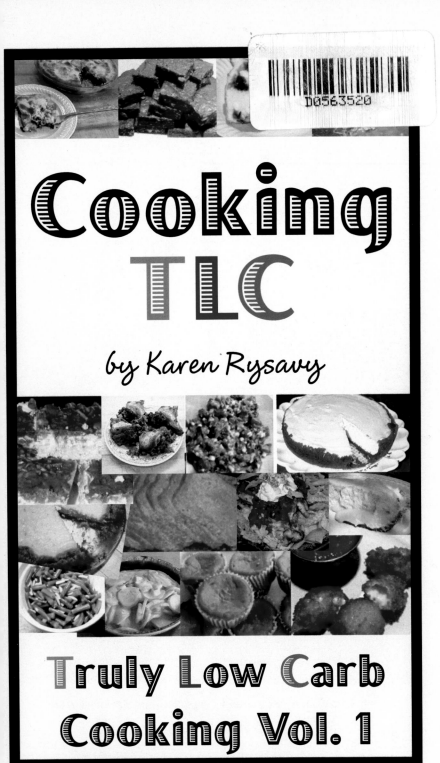

Cooking TLC

by Karen Rysavy

Truly Low Carb Cooking Vol. 1

Visit me on the world wide web at

www.TrulyLowCarb.com

"Because everyone could use a little **TLC!**"

Karen Rysart

Before Low Carb - sickly size 24   One Year Later - healthy size 14

"I will never go back!"

Mustards:	44

Chinese Hot, Sweet Hot, Tasty Jalapeno

Red Ancho Chili Paste	45
Red Relish	46
Seafood Sauce	47
Strawberry Jam	47
Tartar Sauce	48
Teriyaki Marinade & Dipping Sauce	48
Vinegar (Seasoned)	49
Vinaigrettes:	50

Mustard, Raspberry, Garlic Pepper, Sweet and Sour, Sweet Hot

Soups & Main Dishes

Beef Stew	52
Beef Stroganoff	53
Chinese Chicken	54
Chicken Alfredo	55
Chicken Broccoli Strata	56
Chicken Parmesan	57
Clam Chowder	58
Corn Dogs	59
Crab or Lobster Bisque	60
Cream of Vegetable Soup	61
Creamy Seafood Bake	62
Croquettes	63
Egg Drop Soup	65
Fish Fritters	65
Festive Fajita Salad	66
French Onion Soup	67
Green Chili	68
Hot and Sour Soup	69
Impossible Breakfast Pie	70

Mexicali Quiche Variation

Lemon Chicken	71
Meatloaf	72
Meaty Red Chili	73
Nut-Encrusted Fish	74
Radish Greens Soup	75

Vegetables & Side Dishes

Fabulous Fakes: Breads & Sweets

Introduction

Welcome to delicious and nutritious low carb living. I hope that you find my recipes and this book helpful and easy to use. I did my best to keep things simple. If there's a shortcut to take in the kitchen that doesn't sacrifice flavor for convenience, I usually manage to find and incorporate it. But I am very particular about my food - I have one hard and fast rule that I never break: *It has to taste good, or I don't eat it.* It's a good rule to live by.

I also believe in the Low Carb Way of Life with all my heart. The more I research and question and read, the more convinced I become that this really is the path to true health for many, if not most. And it is certainly no sacrifice – to the contrary, low carb eating is infinitely more versatile and satisfying than low fat. You just have to be creative, and it doesn't hurt to be open to new things.

In the relatively short time since I began eating low carb, my tastes have undergone a profound transformation. I enjoy many foods today that I once shunned. The green beans that I used to dislike intensely taste delicate and sweet to me now, and the taste of white sugar and flour makes me recoil in disgust.

You, too, can build a healthier relationship with food. You just have to make a sincere commitment to yourself to *do this*. Do it without cheating for one month. You can do anything for just thirty days! Tell yourself that if you are really not happy at the end of thirty days, you can always change the game plan then. You have nothing to lose but excess weight and/or bad health. And <u>when</u> you make it to day thirty, you will join the ranks of millions of dedicated low carbers like myself who have vowed to never give up the energy and sense of well being that low carb eating brings. At that point, weight loss becomes just a pleasant side effect and this truly becomes a *way of life* instead of a temporary "diet".

I did my best to keep the ingredient list short. Luckily, many or most of the "specialty" ingredients required are readily available in retail stores in many areas already. Given the effectiveness and resulting popularity of low carb eating, I suspect that the availability of low carb products will only continue to improve. That's a mixed blessing — it can make life more convenient, but this Way of Eating (I REFUSE to say diet) works best when you keep your food as simple and natural as possible. Preparing the bulk of your food yourself insures not only that you are eating as healthily as possible, but that you will get the results you want. Designate one day per week for food preparation. Roast pre-marinated meats for thin slicing later, shred and slice the less expensive cuts of bulk cheeses, boil eggs, bake a couple casseroles, a batch of muffins or mini quiches ... portion out nuts, prepare tuna salad, and wash salad vegetables for easy assembly later .... cook bacon or sausage links or patties and freeze them in single servings so you can microwave them fast, later. If you make a commitment to surround yourself with the foods you like from among the many you are free to choose from, so that there's always something for you to grab when you need to, I can almost assure you of success. And if you let yourself run out of convenient choices, I can almost assure you of trouble. Listen to your local Girl Scout — *Always Be Prepared!*

If you need to reduce your overall fat consumption for various health or gastrointestinal reasons, by all means go ahead and substitute reduced fat versions of the ingredients. Everyone reacts differently to different things, we are all individuals, and no one thing works for everyone.

But low carb does work for me, and no matter how crazy the *rest* of my life may be at times, I have discovered that there is at least one area in which I am in complete and total control at all times - and that is: as far as what I put in my mouth and what I do not. I now view food as a source of fuel and health first, and a source of pleasure, last. But, one doesn't necessarily have to preclude the other! And that is what this book is all about.

LEGAL DISCLAIMER: No laboratory analysis has been performed on any of the recipes herein. No guarantee is being made as to the accuracy of these statements and no liability will be assumed for any errors. This book does not attempt to provide complete instructions regarding cooking and safety procedures.

None of the recipes or material herein should be used as, or construed to be, medical advice of any kind. No one should ever undertake any weight loss, nutritional, or exercise program of any kind without prior consultation with, and continual monitoring by, a qualified physician.

IN OTHER WORDS: I did all the recipe analysis myself based on the best information available to me at the time. I cannot personally guarantee the accuracy of the information for individual ingredients, so I certainly can't guarantee that the dish you end up with will exactly match the analysis I provide. As a dieter, it would be best for you to always count your own carbs, calories, etc., based on your own products and their labels.

I expect my readers to be adults who already have a minimum proficiency in the kitchen as well as good old everyday common sense. If you burn yourself while cooking something from this book, or fail to cook, store, or discard something in a timely manner (or in the case of meat, in a "safe" way), that's not my fault! Let's be real, here. This is not a complete how-to-cook manual, *this is just a cookbook*.

This book is not intended to serve as a diet plan or to constitute medical advice of any kind. Please educate yourself about low carb eating by reading and adhering to one of the following plans. Or, read them all and learn things from all of them, as I did, thereby customizing the low carb plan that works best for you. My favorites include: Dr. Atkin's New Diet Revolution, Protein Power Lifeplan, Life Without Bread: How a Low Carbohydrate Diet Can Save Your Life, and the Schwarzbein Principle.

Please see a doctor regularly. As I said before, nothing is right for *everyone* and no one should do this alone. Have lab tests done both before, and during, so your improved results can serve as additional motivation for you in establishing better, healthier eating habits for a lifetime.

Recipe Notes

Splenda™ Granular is the artificial sweetener specified in all of my recipes, except those which only perform well (set up properly) with a sugar alcohol-based (maltitol) syrup.

Wherever my recipes call for something "SF", it stands for "Sugar Free". (This is simply a space consideration.)

Whenever you see a measurement given in grams, it refers to actual weight. If you do not own a food scale, I highly recommend purchasing an accurate model. It makes food preparation and carb counting much easier and quicker, as well as more accurate. All metric conversions have been listed in mls, in order to avoid any confusion between weight versus volume.

My favorite sugar free syrups are made by DaVinci Gourmet™. *Please do not bake with syrups sweetened with aspartame, which is not heat stable.*

I have listed the total carb grams for each recipe when made as directed, as well as total fiber and sugar alcohol grams wherever applicable. You do need to deduct the fiber and/or sugar alcohol grams from the carb grams to arrive at an "effective carb count", if your plan allows for these deductions.

When I list options for a recipe, I analyzed it using the first choice listed.

In recipes that call for protein powder, I am referring to shake mix. I figured carb counts based on using a brand with 3 carbs per cup. I did substitute several different brands in various recipes, and most worked out well, other than a difference in taste between some brands. I recommend a brand that blends soy, whey, and egg protein, for the best baking results. The different textures between brands did cause some small variances in the final products. Please keep in mind that small adjustments in the quantities of protein powder or liquid may be required depending on the brands used, and if you accidentally bake up something with the texture of a tennis ball, a different brand of protein powder may be the cure.

Almond flour, unsweetened coconut, flax seeds, and nut meals are often sold in bulk in the U.S., rarely seem to use a brand name, and often bear no nutrition label (or worse, bear incorrect data). In instances like these, my nutritional counts are based on USDA information and weights/

measures tested personally by Yours Truly. There are many ways to artificially lower the carb count of a recipe - this book does not do so! Carb counts are more often slightly inflated, to allow for regional differences in ingredients. Better safe than sorry, I always say!

Many of my recipes call for vinegar. In recipes which call for cooking after the addition of vinegar, you may substitute an equal amount of wine, if you wish.

Recipes that call for minced garlic were formulated and analyzed using prepared minced garlic, in a jar. You may substitute fresh garlic, but I find the extra work involved is usually not reflected with improved flavor in the finished products, so I do not bother with fresh garlic very often myself. I call for garlic powder in many other recipes, and I have found that the more "granulated" ones work a lot better for me than the brands that actually resemble powder, in so far as their textures.

When a recipe calls for the zest (peel) of a lemon *and* some of its juice, you should of course always use the freshly squeezed juice. If a recipe calls for lemon juice only, I typically use bottled juice with good results. Only go to extra trouble in the kitchen when the taste is directly affected! Otherwise, make it easy on yourself. You will probably find that you enjoy cooking "from scratch" more, and may do it more often.

ThickenThin NotStarch™ continues to thicken with setting, so leftovers and sauces using this ingredient may need to be thinned when reheated, for best results. Guar gum can usually be substituted for NotStarch at the ratio of 1/3 the amount with decent results - if the recipe calls for 3 Tb. NotStarch, you can try substituting 1 Tb. of guar gum, if you wish. *The guar gum is MUCH more likely to lump, so use extreme caution when substituting.*

Baked goods using soy do not keep well for any length of time. I suggest portioning and freezing them promptly. You can then thaw just the amount needed.

Some recipes call for a small amount of chopped onions and I use frozen, pre-chopped onions most of the time. If you can't find the handy chopped frozen onions in your store, or if you just prefer to do this yourself, chop one onion, spread it out on a flat baking sheet in a single layer, then freeze it uncovered for about an hour. Store the pieces in a tightly sealed plastic bag, for long term storage. You will be able to measure out the right amount easily thereafter because the individual pieces will stay separate instead of clumping together. Use the same method for preserving fresh berries, raw diced bell peppers, blanched vegetables, etc., when they are in season and less expensive.

If I call for "cream" in a recipe, use whatever kind you'd like. The small variance in carbs between half and half and whipping cream is usually not enough to affect the average carb count of a single serving. Nutritional data in these instances has been based on using half and half cream.

In some recipes that call for bake mix, I only list one set of nutritional values. In these cases, using any one version of the bake mix resulted in such similar data that I chose not to list it separately.

Freshly ground pepper is ALWAYS best!

Still have questions? Need some extra support? Please visit www.trulylowcarb.com's fun and easy-to-use Message Board on the world wide web.

Nut Flour TLC

I make my almond flour in either a miniature food processor (I own an Oscar™), or in a large high quality food processor (a Cuisinart™). I have successfully used both "whole raw" almonds with the skins still on, and "blanched almonds", which do not have skins and therefore have less fiber and a slightly higher carb count. A small coffee grinder works best for grinding seeds and may be used for nut meals and flours as well.

Just fill the bowl of the machine you are using to the halfway point - no more than that - and pulse the machine on and off until you have a fine consistency. If you must, you can fish out any few stubborn nuts from each batch, rather than over-process the rest. Don't expect a fine powdery flour - your end result will be closer to a "meal" than a true flour - in fact, the terms are often used interchangeably.

My end results work satisfactorily in recipes, and it is definitely both cheaper and fresher to do it this way, but my final take on the matter is this: if time is a big deal, and if you can find what you want, just buy the pre-ground stuff and enjoy it! I find this task to be unnecessarily time consuming, given my schedule. It definitely works, though.

Nut Butter TLC

If you wish to make your own nut butter, I recommend toasting the nuts first at 325 F (165C) for about half an hour, then pureeing them. Adding a little SF syrup in the same flavor as the nuts you are grinding makes it even better. Some nuts work better then others - experiment! Hazelnut remains one of my favorites, with pecan a close second.

Deep Frying TLC:
Tips for Beginning Fry-Cooks

I personally use and recommend grapeseed oil when deep-frying foods, both for its mild flavor and its health benefits (that's grapeseed with a 'g', not to be confused with rapeseed. Rapeseed oil is also known as canola oil, and it is very unstable when heated). Olive oil is great too - if you like the taste. It is important when you are deep frying to use a heavy saucepan with high sides, one my own grandma would likely have called a "vessel". The temperature of the oil that you fry in is crucial to the success of your efforts. If you crowd the pan and reduce the temperature of the oil too much, your end result will be greasy and unappealing. If you let the oil get too hot, the insides won't cook before the outsides char. But, don't worry! It's really easy to get the hang of this, and once you do, you'll always have crispy delicious nibbles. If you're worried about all this or do not have good results the first time you try, you can buy a cheap thermometer that will clip right to the side of your pan. Try to keep the oil at 360 - 380 degrees F (180 - 195 C). For me, a " medium-high" heat setting and letting it pre-heat for a good ten minutes before starting always seems to work perfectly. Line a pan with several layers of paper towels and turn on the oven to 325 degrees F (165 C). Fry just a few items at a time, then put them into the lined pan and into the oven to stay warm while you cook off the rest. It is best not to fry different foods at the same time, and to always fry similar sized portions at one time.

After you are finished eating, strain the cool oil through a mesh colander and refrigerate for reuse. If not reused promptly, discard. Do not reuse oil if any strong odors can be detected, such as may exist after using oil to fry fish.

Appetizers & Snacks

All Purpose / Veggie Dip

- **1 cup sour cream** (240 ml)
- **1 cup mayonnaise** (240 ml)
- **1 Tb. dried parsley** (15 ml)
- **1 tsp. dried minced onion** (5 ml)
- **1 Tb. dried dill weed** (15 ml)
- **1 Tb. Beau Monde™ seasoning** (15 ml, you can substitute Bon Appetit™ or Spike™ seasoning blends, or just use 2 tsp. {10 ml} of celery salt instead).

Just stir ingredients together until thoroughly blended. This is so easy, it is hard to believe it is as good it is! Allow to rest overnight, for best flavor. Serve with low carb crackers, raw vegetables, pork rinds, low carb tortilla "chips", etc.

Per 1/4 cup serving: 265 cal, 30 g fat (7 sat.), 2 g carb, 1 g protein

---

Did you know ...

Fresh lemon juice or baking soda will remove the scent of onions from your hands - but so will rubbing them together under plain running water while holding a piece of stainless steel, such as a table knife.

Avocado Mold

A nice alternative to guacamole when entertaining, this makes for a much more impressive presentation.

- **1 envelope unflavored gelatin** (10 ml, 2 tsp.)
- **½ cup cold water** (120 ml)
- **½ cup boiling water** (120 ml)
- **½ cup heavy cream** (120 ml)
- **½ cup mayonnaise** (120 ml)
- **1 Tb. Red Hot™ or Tabasco™ sauce** (15 ml)
- **2 cups mashed Haas avocados** (4 small or 2 large, usually, 480 ml)

Combine gelatin and cold water and allow to soften for five minutes. Add boiling water to softened gelatin, stir well, and allow to cool thoroughly. Whip cream and set aside. Combine avocados and all other ingredients and pour into well oiled 3-cup (750-ml) mold. Chill thoroughly. To serve, dip mold BRIEFLY into hot water; then invert onto serving platter.

12 servings, each: 162 cal, 15 g fat (4 sat.), 7 g carb (4 g fiber), 1 g protein

---

Did you know ...

To get the most juice out of fresh lemons or oranges, bring them to room temperature and roll them under your palm against the kitchen counter before squeezing.

Cheese Crisps

Popular for years, these are hardly original, but they are a MUST in any low carber's repertoire.

- **1/3 cup semi-hard shredded cheese, such as Cheddar, Colby, Swiss, etc.** (80 ml)

Do not attempt to use very soft cheeses such as Feta, Mozzarella, Brie, etc. Heat a non-stick pan over medium high heat. Sprinkle sliced or finely shredded cheese in a thin layer over the bottom of the entire pan. Okay, are you ready? Here's the big secret: <u>Leave it alone</u> **for several minutes! First it will bubble up all over, then start to look almost lacey (with lots of holes in it); finally you will see clear grease start to run off. When it is lightly golden brown, start carefully teasing up the edges until you can pick it up and turn it over. The second side will cook very quickly in comparison to the first. Drain on clean toweling. Shape into forms or cut into desired shapes before it cools too much. To form a bowl, simply lay over an overturned bowl and gently push the sides down to shape them. Don't burn yourself!**

Per each, made with Mild Cheddar: 120 cal, 10 g fat (6 sat.), 1 g carb, 7 g protein

---

Did you know ...

Cheese should be served at room temperature for maximum flavor.

Chili Cheese Dip

- **½ cup diced canned tomatoes, drained** (120 ml)
- **8 oz. ground beef, cooked and drained** (225 gm)
- **12 slices American cheese**
- **1 Tb. ground cumin** (15 ml)
- **1 tsp. minced garlic** (5 ml)
- **1 tsp. salt** (5 ml)
- **1 Tb. black pepper** (15 ml)
- **1 tsp. cayenne pepper** (5 ml)
- **3 Tb. heavy cream** (45 ml)

Just combine ingredients and heat and stir until melted and smooth. Wonderful for parties; serve in a crock-pot.

Serve with low carb crackers, raw vegetables, pork rinds, low carb tortilla or cheese "chips", etc.

Approx. nine ½-cup servings, each: *176 cal, 13 g fat (7 sat.), 4 g carb, 12 g protein*

Did you know ...

It doesn't take much space to grow your own herb garden in a few pots in a sunny windowsill. Once you start cooking with fresh herbs, though, nothing else will do!

Crab Puffs

- **½ cup softened unsalted butter** (120 ml)
- **10 oz.** (2 jars or 280 gm) **Kraft™ Olde English cheese spread**
- **1 cup cooked crab meat** (240 gm/ml, 6.5 oz., drained)
- **1 tsp. Old Bay™ seasoning** (5 ml, optional)
- **8 bran crackers or Melba toasts**

Cream butter and cheese spread together thoroughly. Gently fold in crab meat, taking care not to break up the lumps too much. Pile high on 8 crackers or Melba toasts. Place on wire rack over a drip pan and broil approximately ten minutes, until well browned and bubbly. Remove from rack and cut each cracker or toast into bite size pieces.

8 servings - I think these are best on white Melba toasts, if your carb counts allow.

For crab topping only, not including cracker base, each: 222 cal, 21 g fat (12 sat.), < 1 g carb, 9 g protein

---

Did you know ...

Clogged drain? Try this: Drop three effervescent denture tablets down the drain followed by a cup of white vinegar - Wait a few minutes, then run the hot water. A non-toxic and affordable first line of defense!

Crackers: Bran Rounds

- ¼ **cup cold unsalted butter** (60 ml)
- **2 cups grated sharp cheddar** (480 ml)
- **½ cup grated Parmesan cheese** (120 ml)
- **1 tsp. garlic powder** (5 ml)
- **1 tsp. Worcestershire Sauce** (5 ml)
- **1 tsp. black pepper** (5 ml)
- **1 cup soy flour** (240 ml, may use other flours)
- **½ cup vital wheat gluten** (120 ml)
- **1½ cups wheat bran** (360 ml)
- **½ cup flax meal** (120 ml)
- **½ cup oat bran** (120 ml)
- **½ - 1 cup water** (120-240 ml)
- **½ tsp. salt** (2.5 ml)

Preheat oven to 400 degrees F (200 C). Place the cold butter, half the cheddar cheese, the Parmesan, garlic powder, and Worcestershire sauce into a food processor. Pulse until well incorporated and mealy. Add salt, pepper, soy flour, wheat gluten, wheat bran, flax seed and oat bran and pulse until mixed well. Pour into a large bowl. Add remaining cheddar. Add water, one tablespoon full at a time, and work it in with your hands, until mixture is easily packed into balls that hold together easily. Do not get it too wet! Use a tablespoon measure to scoop out even portions of dough. Using the palm of your hand, flatten balls of dough directly onto a very well-greased or parchment paper-lined cookie sheet, or flatten with a tortilla press. Smooth any cracks that form in the edges with your fingers. Bake at 400 degrees until browned, about 15 minutes, then reduce heat and bake at 300 degrees for another 15 minutes. Immediately remove from cookie sheet and cool on wire racks.

36 crackers, each: 93 cal, 6 g fat (3 g sat.), 4 g carb (2 g fiber), 5 g protein

Crackers: Easy Cheese Wafers

- **½ cup water** (120 ml)
- **2 Tb. unsalted butter** (30 ml)
- **¼ cup soy flour** (60 ml, can use other flours)
- **2 Tb. vital wheat gluten** (30 ml)
- **3 oz. extra sharp cheddar cheese** (85 gm)
- **½ tsp. salt** (2.5 ml)
- **¼ cup Parmesan cheese** (60 ml)
- **2 egg whites**

Preheat oven to 400 degrees F (200 C). Bring water and butter to a boil.

Add cheeses, stirring constantly until it melts. Add flours and salt all at once and cook and stir until thickened and bubbly. Remove from heat and allow to cool while you beat egg whites until stiff.

Fold stiff egg whites into cooled cracker mixture gently. Spoon out by the teaspoonful, one inch apart, onto heavily greased or parchment paper-lined baking sheets. Bake at 400 degrees for 15 minutes, till golden; then reduce oven temperature to 300 degrees F (150 C) and bake for an additional 15 minutes, until thoroughly dry and crispy. Cool on racks and seal tightly once completely cooled.

30 crackers, each: 28 cal, 2 g fat (1 g sat.), < 1 g carb, 1 g protein

---

Did you know ...

Place a fabric softener sheet in your gym shoes overnight and they'll smell great in the morning.

Crackers: Easy Dipping Wedges

- **½ cup water** (120 ml)
- **2 Tb. unsalted butter** (30 ml)
- **½ cup oat flour** (120 ml)
- **2 Tb. vital wheat gluten** (30 ml)
- **2 oz. sharp cheddar cheese** (60 gm)
- **½ tsp. salt** (2.5 ml)
- **1 tsp. paprika** (5 ml)
- **¼ tsp. seasoned salt** (1.25 ml)

Preheat oven to 400 degrees F (200 C). Bring water and butter to a boil. Add cheese, stirring constantly until it is melted. Add flours and salt all at once and stir. Mixture should immediately form a large ball. Turn out onto cutting board and cut into equal wedge shaped pieces. Sprinkle heavily on both sides with paprika and lightly on one side with seasoned salt. Bake on heavily greased or parchment paper-lined baking sheets for 15 minutes, till browned; then reduce oven temperature to 300 degrees F (150 C) and bake for an additional 15 minutes, until thoroughly dry and crispy. Cool on racks and seal tightly once completely cooled.

16 crackers, each: 56 cal, 4 g fat (2 g sat.), 1 g carb, 2 g protein

For extra zip, sprinkle any of the crackers with curry powder, or with garlic powder, cracked black pepper and some cayenne pepper before baking. Experiment! You could do a sweet cinnamon and Splenda combination, etc. The above dough is good when rolled thinly and deep-fried instead of baked, too.

If crackers become stale, place in a slow oven (300 degrees F or 150 C) for about 20 minutes.

Deep-Fried Cheese & Veggies

- **Mozzarella "string" cheese sticks, cut into approximately 2" lengths**
- **Sliced zucchini, eggplant, summer squash, broccoli and cauliflower florets, asparagus, green beans, ETC!**
- **Eggs**
- *TLC Bake Mix*
- **Water**
- **Parmesan cheese**
- **A mild flavored oil for frying** - I recommend grapeseed or extra-virgin olive oil.

Mix breading batter as follows: 1 egg to each ¼ cup (60 ml) of bake mix. How much you mix will depend on how much you plan to make. Add 1 tsp. water to egg and bake mix, then add additional water 1 tsp. at a time until batter reaches the proper consistency (when you dip an item in it, it should coat the outside thoroughly without being *too* thick). Depending on the humidity in your area, you may need to add a little more or less water to get it just right. Pierce each item with a toothpick and dip into batter. Hold above bowl and allow any excess batter to run off, then roll it in grated Parmesan cheese, and deep fry in hot oil until golden brown, turning once. You will need to cook the vegetables longer than the cheese, which cooks very quickly. Total cooking time depends on the thickness and type of vegetable. Drain on paper towels and serve with dipping sauces. I like to serve the cheese stix with Marinara sauce and the veggies with ranch.

Carbs and nutritional data will vary w i d e l y, depending on ingredients used. An average serving of 2 fried string cheese sticks would equal 320 calories, 27 g fat (10 g sat.), 3 g carb, 19 g protein.

Beginning Fry Cooks refer to *Deep Frying TLC*, pg 14.

Garlic Pepper Jerky

- **3 lb. round or rump beef roast, flank steak, or London Broil** (or use turkey, chicken, pork, etc. When using beef, I ask the store to slice it for me "thinly, cross-grain" - 1350 gm)
- **1½ cups Worcestershire sauce** (360 ml)
- **1 Tb. molasses** (15 ml)
- **1 Tb. liquid smoke** (15 ml)
- **3 Tb. SF maple syrup** (45 ml)
- **2 Tb. garlic powder** (30 ml)
- **1 Tb. onion powder** (15 ml)
- **1½ tsp. ground cumin** (7.5 ml)
- **¼ cup white vinegar** (60 ml)
- **1 tsp. cayenne pepper** (5 ml, or more, to taste)
- **2 Tb. black pepper** (30 ml)
- **2 tsp. paprika** (10 ml)
- **2 Tb. ThickenThin NotStarch™** (30 ml - optional but very good when included)
- **2 Tb. oil** (30 ml - I use Mongolian Fire Oil)

Remove visible fat from meat. Mix liquid ingredients together, pour over pre-sliced meat, and marinate in refrigerator for 24-48 hours. (For even coverage, I usually dip each piece of meat in the marinade, and layer, then pour the remaining marinade over all.) Jerky is best when made in a commercial dehydrator. They are widely available and not expensive, when compared to the price of pre-made jerky. I urge you to get one, but you can make this recipe in your conventional oven, as well. Just drape meat slices over pre-oiled racks (for easy clean up later) place over drip trays and bake at lowest oven temperature, usually 200 degrees F (95 C), at least overnight, or for as long as several days, depending on the thickness of the meat. Make sure you cook it long enough! When using a commercial dehydrator, follow the manufacturer's instructions.

Using eye of round and with yield of 48: 57 cal, 2 g fat, 1 g carb, 8 g protein, each.

25

Guacamole

- **2 medium pitted Haas avocados**
- **1 Tb. fresh lemon or lime juice** (15 ml)
- **1 tsp. garlic powder** (5 ml)
- **1 tsp. Splenda™ Granular** (5 ml)
- **2 Tb. sour cream** (optional - 30 ml)
- **½ tsp. salt** (2.5 ml)

Classic guacamole has always been easy to make and is naturally low carb. I dice one of the avocados and mash the other one. Mix everything together, and serve immediately. (I like it better without the sour cream, personally).

6 servings, each: 126 cal, 10 g fat (2 g sat.), 9 g carb (5 g fiber), 1 g protein

Hot Spinach Dip

- **2 Tb. unsalted butter** (30 ml)
- **1/3 cup diced onions** (80 ml)
- **10 oz. frozen spinach** (280 gm)
- **6 oz. bacon, cooked and crumbled** (170 gm)
- **4 oz. cream cheese** (115 gm)
- **2 Tb. heavy cream** (30 ml)
- **½ cup mozzarella** (120 ml)
- **½ cup shredded cheddar** (120 ml)
- **½ cup pork rind crumbs** (about 1 oz or 30 gm)

Squeeze all water out of thawed spinach. Sauté onions in butter until caramelized (very browned). Stir in cream cheese and cream and heat until smooth. Add spinach and blend. Place in ovenproof pan with shallow sides and cover with shredded cheeses, pork rind crumbs, and crumbled bacon. Broil until heated through, bubbly, and browned.

6 servings, each: 365 cal, 30 g fat (9 g sat.), 3 g carb (1 g fiber), 20 g protein

Lazy Five-Day Pickled Cukes And Zukes

- **3 average cucumbers** (24 oz. or 675 gm)
- **3 average zucchinis** (15 oz. or 420 gm)
- **24 pearl onions or 2 bunches green onions**
- **4 cups white vinegar** (1 liter)
- **4 cups Splenda™ Granular** (1 liter)
- **1 tsp. ground turmeric** (5 ml)
- **1½ tsp. celery seeds** (7.5 ml)
- **1½ tsp. mustard seeds** (7.5 ml)
- **1 Tb. dried onion flakes** (15 ml)
- **1 Tb. whole black peppercorns** (15 ml)
- **½ cup Kosher or pickling salt** (120 ml)

Wash and slice cucumbers and zucchinis into evenly sized pieces. Peel pearl onions by blanching in boiling water for 3 minutes, then cutting off ends and removing skins. If using green onions, slice into 1-inch pieces. Layer vegetables into a clean glass gallon size jar. Mix vinegar, Splenda™, and spices together; pour over vegetables. Place in refrigerator and stir or shake at least once a day for five straight days before eating. Best after sitting for a whole month. The vegetables will shrink as they cure, and there will be more than enough liquid.

When the vegetables are all gone, you can reuse the brine solution to make another batch. You can substitute all sorts of vegetables in this recipe. Substitute fresh dill for the turmeric and mustard seeds if you prefer a dill flavor. Add hot peppers such as jalapenos and habaneras, or pickle cauliflower florets, asparagus spears, hard boiled eggs, beet and turnip slices...

72 servings, each: 11 cal, 2 g carb - assuming you consumed the liquid too, which is highly unlikely, and which contains the bulk of the carbs.

Picante Sauce

- **1 cup finely chopped, fresh tomatoes** (240 ml)
- **14 oz. can of diced tomatoes, with juices** (400 gm)
- **2 Tb. minced green onions** (30 ml)
- **2 Tb. minced fresh cilantro** (30 ml - may add more or less, to taste, I use 4-6 Tb.)
- **½ Haas avocado, diced** (optional - about 150 gm)
- **1 Tb. fresh lime juice** (15 ml)
- **1 Tb. Splenda™ Granular** (15 ml)
- **¼ tsp. salt** (1.25 ml)
- **2 tsp. black pepper** (10 ml)
- **1 tsp. ground cumin** (5 ml)
- **½ tsp. celery salt** (2.5 ml)
- **½ tsp. chili powder** (2.5 ml)
- **1 oz. chopped black olives** (optional - 30 gm)
- **1 roasted minced hot jalapeno or habanera pepper** OR **1 Tb. hot pepper sauce** (15 ml)
- **2 tsp. ThickenThin NotStarch™** (optional - 10 ml)

Combine all ingredients in a large bowl and allow flavors to combine for at least a couple hours before serving. Keeps in refrigerator for 4-7 days.

VARIATIONS: If not using NotStarch™, I recommend straining off the juices (save them to use when seasoning ground beef for taco salads or wraps?) You may use all canned tomatoes (2 cans total) with excellent results, or use 2 cans Mexican-style canned tomatoes (I prefer Rotel™) and skip the lime juice and green chilies.

12 servings, each about 1/2 cup: 33 cal, 2 g fat (0 g sat.), 4 g carb (1 g fiber)

Pickled Peppers

It is crucial that all steps be followed to the letter (*"Can you say: botulism?"*) But don't let an irrational fear of food poisoning prevent you from learning to can food – it is completely safe, as long as you follow directions.

EQUIPMENT AND SUPPLIES REQUIRED

- **Water Bath Canner & Rack**
- **Canning Jars: Quart size, reusable. Buy any brand labeled "for home canning". Wide mouth jars are easier for a novice to pack, and are recommended for this project.**
- **Jar Rings and New Canning Seals (flats): Included with new jars, and inexpensively replaced. Never reuse the flat seals. Rings can be reused indefinitely as long as they are not rusty or out of shape.**
- **Canning Tongs and Plastic Spatula**
- **Rubber Gloves and Safety Glasses**
- **Peppers: Jalapeno, habanera, chili, Serrano, cherry - whatever flavor and heat level you prefer. (I use jalapenos.)**
- **Extras: Strips of bell pepper, sliced zucchini, cauliflower, and cucumbers make nice additions to (or substitutions for) peppers.**
- **Whole Peppercorns**
- **Coarse Kosher or Pickling Salt**
- **White Vinegar**
- **Garlic (2-3 cloves per quart)**

Wash peppers well. Pierce each one 2-3 times with a sharp knife. Cover with salt water brine (water mixed with 3 Tb. {45 ml} pickling salt per quart) and leave to soak overnight.

Wash jars, lids, and flats with hot soapy water. Sterilize jars: place them in a clean canner and cover with 2" of water. Bring to a gentle boil, and then begin timing. Boil for 15 minutes plus 1 additional minute for each 1000 feet of elevation above sea level. Remove jars from hot water

(recipe continued next page)

using canning tongs, and drain.

Drain peppers. Prepare "extras" as needed. (Peel, wash, slice into strips, etc.)

Add 1 tsp. (5 ml) **pickling salt, 1 Tb.** (15 ml) **whole peppercorns, and 2 - 3 whole peeled cloves or ¼-½ tsp.** (1.25 –2.5 ml) **minced garlic to each jar.**

DON YOUR GLOVES AND SAFETY GLASSES. Pack the jars with vegetables. Pack only 7 jars at a time, per canner. You should push the peppers into the jars firmly, but don't crush them. Alternate the direction of the stems to fill the jar more evenly. Leave 2" at the top of the jar empty. I usually pack the peppers in vertically, then wedge a couple in at the top horizontally. This is when you'll be grateful for the safety glasses – salty, peppery brine can squirt all the way across the room while you are doing this! (If any gets on your skin, wash the affected area immediately with soapy water.)

Mix white vinegar and water in equal amounts, and fill the jars to within ½" of the top, making sure to cover the contents completely. I often have to remove a few peppers at this point, or occasionally even add one.

Take the flexible plastic spatula and run it up and down between the peppers and the glass, all the way around. This removes extra air from the jars and insures a good seal. You may find yourself re-packing a couple jars at this point and adding more liquid. If so, be sure to repeat the spatula drill. (Once this is all done, feel free to remove the glasses and gloves.)

Take a damp paper towel and clean the top lip of each jar. Center a flat lid on each jar and twist the rings on. Don't tighten them too much, just enough to keep things in place. The actual seal comes from the water bath processing. Place the canning rack and jars in the empty canner.

Cover the jars with 2" of water, cover, bring to a simmer, then begin timing. Process quart jars for

15 minutes plus one minute for each 1,000 feet in elevation above sea level. Remove jars with canning tongs and gently place on a rack or clean towel, leaving room in between each jar. As the jars cool, they will seal. Once cool, inspect each jar for a tight seal. Refrigerate after opening. *Nutritional counts will vary widely depending on actual ingredients and quantities used - I count these as 5 calories and 1 carb each.*

Red Pepper Hummus

- **1 medium sweet red pepper** (about 4 oz, or 100 gm)
- **10 oz. silken style soft tofu** (280 gm)
- **1 Tb. white vinegar** (15 ml)
- **2 tsp. olive oil** (10 ml)
- **1 tsp. minced garlic** (5 ml)
- **½ tsp. salt** (2.5 ml)
- **1 tsp. black pepper** (5 ml)
- **1 roasted hot jalapeno or habanera pepper**
- **1½ oz. feta cheese** (40 gm)

Roast one red bell pepper and jalapeno or habanera under broiler or on top of gas range, or even on a grill, until skin is completely blackened and charred. Cool slightly and place in a heavy-duty plastic bag; allow to rest for 20 minutes. Remove blackened skin, stem, and seeds. (When working with hot peppers, wear gloves to do this. And eye protection is a good idea, too.) Place in blender or food processor with remaining ingredients and puree, scraping down sides at least once. Remember that chilling dulls flavors, and adjust seasonings accordingly. You want the spices stronger at this point than they need to be. That way, the final product will taste right once it is thoroughly chilled. This is best when made a day ahead, to allow flavors to meld properly. Delicious with pork rinds and celery stick dippers.

8 servings, each: 53 cal, 4 g fat (0 g sat.), 2 g carb, 2 g protein

Roast Pepper Pinwheels

- **6 assorted color bell peppers – red, green, yellow, orange...** (600 gm)
- **8 oz. softened cream cheese** (225 gm)
- **2 Tb. minced green onions** (30 ml)
- **1 tsp. minced garlic** (5 ml)
- **2 tsp. Worcestershire sauce** (10 ml)
- **½ tsp. salt** (2.5 ml)
- **1 tsp. black pepper** (5 ml)
- **1 Tb. dried parsley** (30 ml)
- **2 Tb. minced black olives** (optional - 30 ml)
- **1 minced fresh seeded jalapeno or habanera pepper** (optional, OR 1 Tb. hot pepper sauce, 15 ml)

Roast peppers directly over gas flame, under broiler, or on grill until skin is completely blackened. Cool slightly and place in heavy-duty plastic bag. Allow to rest in bag for twenty minutes; peel skin from peppers and remove seeds. Cut peppers in two pieces each. Square up edges and mince and reserve the trimmings. Chill pepper squares before proceeding. Mix softened cream cheese with onions, garlic, Worcestershire sauce, salt, pepper, parsley, olives, minced jalapenos, and reserved minced roasted peppers.

Spread cheese mixture over the 12 pepper pieces. Starting with the short end, roll up each pepper jellyroll fashion. Slice pepper rolls about ¼ inch thick and arrange on a platter. Colorful as well as tasty, these are great make ahead party appetizers that can be easily customized for a theme – use mixed red and green peppers for a Christmas party, red peppers with alternating regular white filling and tinted blue filling on the 4th of July, orange peppers at Halloween, etc.

12 servings , each: 77 cal, 7 g fat (4 g sat.), 2 g carb, 2 g protein

Spicy Nut Mix

- **4 cups mixed nuts** (1 liter - I prefer a mixture of macs, almonds and walnuts but you can use any mix of nuts and seeds.)
- **½ cup melted butter** (120 ml)
- **2 Tb. Worcestershire sauce** (30 ml)
- **1 tsp. cayenne pepper** (5 ml)
- **1½ tsp. garlic powder** (7.5 ml)
- **1 tsp. onion powder** (5 ml)

Melt butter and mix with spices and Worcestershire sauce. Place nuts in a 13" x 9" pan. Pour butter mixture over all and stir thoroughly. Bake at 275 degrees F (135 C) for one hour, stirring every fifteen minutes. Allow to drain and cool over a layer of clean towels.

8 servings, 482 cal, 48 g fat (11 g sat.), 10 g carb (5 g fiber), 9 g protein, each.

Sweet Nut Crunch

- **4 cups mixed nuts** (1 liter - I prefer a mixture of filberts, pecans, and walnuts but you can use any mix of nuts and seeds.)
- **½ cup dried cranberries or tart cherries** (unsweetened, 120 ml , about 2 oz. or 60 gm)
- **½ cup melted butter** (120 ml)
- **1 cup Splenda™ Granular** (240 ml)
- **½ cup unsweetened coconut** (120 ml - flaked works better than grated, in this recipe)
- **1 Tb. vanilla extract** (15 ml)

Prepare as described above for *Spicy Nut Mix.*
Just a little of this mix can do wonders to perk up plain low carb cereal or yogurt!

16 servings, each: 241 cal, 23 g fat (5 g sat.), 7 g carb, 3 g protein. If you omit the fruit, the same serving has just 5 g carb.

Teriyaki Jerky

- **3 lbs. lean beef round roast or flank steak, etc.** (or you could use turkey, chicken, pork, etc. When using beef, I have the store slice it for me "thinly, cross-grain" - 1350 gm)
- **½ cup soy sauce** (120 ml)
- **½ cup Liquid Aminos** (120 ml, may use additional soy sauce if you can't find the aminos)
- **½ cup 0-carb SF maple syrup** (120 ml)
- **1 Tb. liquid smoke** (15 ml)
- **1 Tb. dry mustard** (15 ml)
- **1 Tb. red wine vinegar** (15 ml)
- **1 Tb. ThickenThin NotStarch™** (15 ml - optional but recommended for very best results)
- **1 Tb. garlic powder** (15 ml)
- **2 Tb. oil** (30 ml)

Remove visible fat from meat. Mix liquid ingredients together, pour over pre-sliced meat, and marinate in refrigerator for 24-48 hours. (For even coverage, I usually dip each piece of meat in the marinade, and layer, then pour the remaining marinade over all.) Jerky is best when made in a commercial dehydrator. They are widely available and not expensive, when compared to the price of pre-made jerky. I urge you to get one, but you can make this recipe in your conventional oven, as well. Just drape meat slices over pre-oiled racks (for easy clean up later) place over trays and bake at lowest oven temperature, usually 200 degrees F (95 C), at least overnight, or for as long as several days, depending on the thickness of the meat. Make sure you cook it long enough! When using a commercial dehydrator, follow the manufacturer's instructions.

Using eye of round and with yield of 48: 57 cal, 2 g fat, 0 g carb, 8 g protein, each.

Condiments & Sauces

Barbecue Sauce

- **6 oz. tomato paste** (170 gm)
- **8 oz. tomato puree or sauce** (225 gm)
- **½ cup red wine vinegar** (120 ml)
- **2 Tb. Splenda™ Granular** (30 ml)
- **1 Tb. black pepper** (15 ml)
- **1 Tb. dry parsley** (15 ml)
- **1 Tb. blackstrap molasses** (15 ml)
- **¼ tsp. ground cloves** (1.25 ml)
- **1/3 cup SF maple flavor syrup** (80 ml)
- **½ tsp. cinnamon** (2.5 ml)
- **¼ tsp. allspice** (1.25 ml)
- **1 tsp. paprika** (5 ml)
- **½ tsp. garlic powder** (2.5 ml)
- **½ tsp. celery salt** (2.5 ml)
- **2 tsp. liquid smoke** (10 ml)
- **1 tsp. cayenne pepper** (5 ml, optional)

Whisk all ingredients together in a saucepan and heat until flavors are well mixed and sauce is smooth and without lumps.

You can leave out the cinnamon and allspice, but I wish you'd try it this way at least once. Their inclusion was one of those happy kitchen accidents that I ended up enjoying a lot, and I think you will too.

Per 2 Tb: 10 cal, 2 g carb

Did you know ...

fabric softener sheets will clean baked-on food from a cooking pan? Put a sheet in the pan, fill with water, let sit overnight, and sponge clean. The anti-static agents apparently weaken the bond between the food and the pan while the fabric softening agents soften the baked-on food.

Berri-Licious Syrup

- **3 cups chopped berries and low carb fruits of your choice** (720 ml—I I enjoy combinations of rhubarb, blueberry, strawberry, peach, blackberry and/or raspberry.)
- **1 cup SF vanilla syrup** (240 ml)
- **4 Tb. ThickenThin NotStarch™** (60 ml)
- **2 tsp. lemon juice** (10 ml)
- **4 Tb. water** (60 ml)
- **½ tsp. ground cinnamon** (2.5 ml)

Bring fruit and syrup to a boil, then lower heat and simmer, covered, until fruit is very soft. Pass through a sieve or food mill to remove any fibrous portions of rhubarb and/or seeds from berries; return strained liquid to saucepan. Stir NotStarch™ into water. Add cinnamon and lemon juice. Add to saucepan and whisk over low heat until smooth and thickened.

A half blueberry, half rhubarb combination, per 1/4 cup: 28 cal, 0.1 g fat, 6 g carb (3 g fiber)

If it gets too thick after refrigeration, simply warm it slightly in the microwave and add water as needed. Eat over pancakes, waffles, puddings, pies, cakes, ice cream, etc. This recipe originally called for NotSugar, but I think either product works equally as well here.

Did you know ...

One lemon usually yields about 1/4 cup of juice and one orange should yield about 1/3 cup.

Bleu Cheese Dressing

- **2 cups mayonnaise** (480 ml)
- **¾ cup buttermilk** (180 ml)
- **4 oz. crumbled bleu cheese** (115 gm)
- **1 tsp. garlic powder** (5 ml)

Mix it up and let it sit for 24 hours before using.
Per 2 Tb: 155 cal, 16 g fat (3 g sat.), 0 g carb, 1 g protein

Buttermilk Ranch

- **¾ cup mayonnaise** (180 ml)
- **1 cup buttermilk** (240 ml)
- **½ tsp. garlic powder** (2.5 ml)
- **1 Tb. dried parsley** (15 ml)
- **½ tsp. celery salt** (2.5 ml)
- **½ tsp. onion powder** (2.5 ml)
- **1 Tb. white vinegar** (15 ml)
- **1 Tb. Splenda™ Granular** (15 ml)

Whisk it all together and enjoy!

Per 2 Tb: 150 cal, 14 g fat (2 g sat.), 1 g carb

(Good with reduced fat substitutes also.)

Did you know ...

Adding 2 Tb. (30 ml) **of white vinegar to the water when boiling fish will make it sweeter and more tender?**

Catsup

- **6 oz. tomato paste** (170 gm)
- **15 oz. can tomato sauce** (420 gm)
- **1 cup water** (240 ml)
- **½ cup cider vinegar** (120 ml)
- **½ cup Splenda™ Granular** (120 ml)
- **1 tsp. paprika** (5 ml)
- **2 Tb. ThickenThin NotStarch™** (30 ml)
- **½ tsp. black pepper** (2.5 ml)
- **½ tsp. salt** (2.5 ml)
- **smidgen ground cloves** (0.5 ml)
- **smidgen ground cinnamon** (0.5 ml)
- **dash allspice** (1 ml)
- **¼ tsp. garlic powder** (1.25 ml)

Whisk all ingredients together in a saucepan and heat until flavors are well mixed and sauce is smooth and without lumps.

When I say smidgen, I mean you should take the smallest measuring spoon you own, usually ¼ or ½ tsp., and fill it only ¼ full! And yes, that tiny amount still makes a difference. For a dash, fill that smallest one ½ full.

Per 2 Tb: 10 cal, 2 g carb

Did you know ...

Spray your plastic storage containers with nonstick cooking spray or oil before pouring in tomato-based sauces, to prevent stains.

Creamy Italian Parmesan Dressing & Marinade

- **¾ cup** *TLC Seasoned Vinegar* (180 ml)
- **½ cup grated Parmesan cheese** (120 ml)
- **1 Tb. sour cream** (15 ml)
- **1 Tb. Splenda™ Granular** (15 ml)
- **2 tsp. Italian seasoning** (10 ml)
- **1 Tb. minced garlic** (15 ml)
- **1 tsp. black pepper** (5 ml)
- **¼ tsp. sea salt** (1.25 ml)
- **1 cup extra virgin olive oil** (240 ml)

(If you can't find "Italian seasoning" in the stores where you live, you can mix your own using equal parts of marjoram, thyme, rosemary, savory, sage, oregano and basil.)

Put everything except the olive oil in a blender or food processor and process until well mixed.

Add ¼ cup (60 ml) **of the olive oil and blend for a full minute. Then add another ¼ cup of the oil, blend, and so on, until all the oil is well incorporated and the mixture has emulsified.** *Don't rush this step.*

Per 2 Tb: 134 cal, 14 g fat (2 g sat.), 0 g carb, 1 g protein

Try this as a poultry marinade and grilling sauce. Omit the Parmesan when using as a marinade. Excellent with Romano cheese instead, and you could always substitute other types of vinegar for the Seasoned.

Horseradish

- **Fresh horseradish roots**
- **White distilled vinegar**

This couldn't be any easier. You do need a food processor, and fresh horseradish roots. If you don't know where there is any growing, ask at your grocer. You can often find fresh roots for sale near the ginger. Wash and scrape/peel roots very well. (Use caution, fumes are hot.) Add 1-2 cups of vinegar to the bowl of a food processor and add one-inch pieces of root, filling no more than one third full. Puree mixture until consistency is very fine, and pack into small jars, pouring off any excess vinegar. May also be made with a traditional grinder, but I find that a high quality food processor does just as good a job, with less fuss and mess. Small jars are best because it keeps better when tightly sealed – the more times it is opened, the less bite it will have.

If you find this too hot for your taste, you can cut the heat by adding ground turnips.

Very low in carbs and calories - I count it as zero.

Creamy Horseradish Sauce

- **¼ cup grated fresh horseradish root** (60 ml)
- **½ cup mayonnaise** (120 ml)
- **2 Tb. sour cream** (30 ml)
- **1 tsp. lemon juice** (5 ml)
- **salt and pepper**

Whisk all ingredients together and add salt and pepper to taste.

Per 2 Tb: 176 cal, 17 g fat (2 g sat.), 0 g carb, 1 g protein

Marinara Sauce

- **2 cups tomato sauce** (480 ml)
- **2 cups diced canned tomatoes, with juice** (480 ml)
- **½ - 1 Tb. minced garlic** (7 – 15 ml)
- **1 Tb. Italian Seasoning** (15 ml, mixed dried marjoram, parsley, savory, thyme, oregano & sage)
- **1 Tb. red wine vinegar** (15 ml)
- **1 Tb. Splenda™ Granular** (15 ml)
- **½ cup Parmesan cheese** (120 ml)

This couldn't be easier, and it tastes great. Just simmer all ingredients together for a few minutes to an hour, over medium heat.
Use on pizzas with cheese crisp crusts, in lasagna dishes, over low carb pasta, and as a dipping sauce for deep-fried cheese and veggie sticks.
Per half cup serving: 53 cal, 1.5 g fat (0 g sat.), 5 g carb, 3 g protein

---

Did you know ...

When you make a casserole, you should consider making an extra one or two for the freezer. It won't take you any longer and you'll then have a meal that you can just take out and pop in the oven whenever you want. You may have to increase baking time by up to 50% when cooking from frozen, but in most cases the dish will taste as good as if you had just put it together that afternoon. Line your dish with foil or plastic wrap, so you can remove the casserole dish while frozen, (for easier storage) then replace it for baking (remove wrap before baking).

Mixed Fruit Jelly

- **1 cup frozen blueberries** (240 ml)
- **1 cup frozen blackberries** (240 ml)
- **1 cup frozen rhubarb** (240 ml)
- **1 envelope plain gelatin** (10 gm, 2 tsp.)
- **Water and/or Fruit-flavored SF syrup**

Put berries and rhubarb in a large stockpot or Dutch oven, over medium heat. Add 1/3 cup water. When berries have thawed sufficiently, crush. Continue to heat berries until completely soft. Put berry mixture through a food mill, or force through a sieve, to remove seeds. Measure remaining juice, and add water or SF syrup if necessary, to increase volume to 1¾ cups (420 ml). Return to stockpot and stir in gelatin. Bring to a full rolling boil, stirring constantly. (A rolling boil is one that does not slow or stop when stirred vigorously.) Continue to boil for exactly one minute; then remove from heat. Allow to cool for another minute, then skim off foam from surface. (Save this for the chef's sample, there is nothing wrong with this so far as taste goes, it just looks funny if left in the jelly.) Pour the jelly into glass jars or plastic containers, wipe rims, close lids, and refrigerate. This makes a tart and lively jelly, perfect for my no-longer-quite-so-sweet sweet tooth. Splenda™ may be added to the original berry mixture if a sweeter end product is desired. You should taste as you go, and adjust the sweetness to your own individual preference.

Heat a small amount of this jelly with a little bit of water to make a delicious topping for low carb ice cream, cheesecake, pancakes, or make a luscious smoothie by blending with ice, water, diet lemon lime soda pop, and heavy cream.

Use within 4 weeks. Freeze if longer storage is required.

Per 2 Tb. serving: 11 cal, 0.1 g fat (0 g sat.), 2 g carb

Can use other combinations of fruit, whatever you like, to measure 3 cups - variations may affect carb count. **43**

Chinese Hot Mustard

- **3 Tb. hot dry yellow mustard** (45 ml)
- **2 Tb. water** (30 ml)
- **1 Tb. soy sauce** (15 ml)

Per Tb: 2 cal, 0 fat, 0.5 g carb, 0 protein

Sweet Hot Mustard

- **1½ cups mayonnaise** (360 ml)
- **½ cup yellow mustard** (120 ml)
- **½ cup white vinegar** (120 ml)
- **¼ cup Splenda™ Granular** (60 ml)
- **1 Tb. cayenne pepper** (15 ml - optional)

Simply whisk ingredients for either of the above mustards together until well mixed and smooth.

Per 2 Tb : 122 cal, 13 g fat (2 g sat.), 0 g carb, 0 g protein

Tasty Jalapeno Mustard

- **1½ cups yellow mustard** (360 ml)
- **6 cocktail onions** (1 oz, 30 gm)
- **2 Tb. diced jalapenos** (30 ml)
- **1 dill pickle spear** (1 oz, 30 gm.)
- **3 Tb. olive oil** (45 ml)
- **3 Tb. Splenda™ Granular** (45 ml)
- **1 tsp. salt** (5 ml)
- **2 tsp. minced garlic** (10 ml)
- **1/3 cup water** (80 ml)
- **1 Tb. onion powder** (15 ml)
- **2 tsp. black pepper** (10 ml)

Combine ingredients in a blender and puree completely. Not too hot, with great flavor.

Per 2 Tb : 24 cal, 2 g fat (0 g sat.), 1 g carb, 0 g protein

Dressing Variation: Mix 1 cup jalapeno mustard with equal amount of white vinegar; add 3 Tb. Splenda, or to taste. *Per 2 Tb: 13 cal, 1 g fat (0 g sat.), 0 g carb*

Red Ancho Chili Paste

- **2 dried Red Ancho chili peppers** (sometimes called just 'New Mexico peppers')
- **6 small red hot peppers** (Mine were called Chili Pequin but any small, hot, dried red pepper will do.)
- **1 cup water** (240 ml)
- **1 tsp. minced garlic** (5 ml)
- **1 tsp. ground oregano** (5 ml)
- **1 Tb. ground cumin** (15 ml)
- **2 tsp. black pepper** (10 ml)
- **½ tsp. salt** (2.5 ml)
- **2 Tb. olive oil** (30 ml)

Rip open all peppers and discard the seeds and stems.
Warm the water and put it in blender with the peppers. Allow to soak for at least one hour.
Add remaining ingredients and blend until smooth.

Makes a wonderful seasoning for fajitas, tacos, and taco salads. Not too spicy for the kids, still enough flavor for the adults. Add to soups, casseroles, and sauces.

Per 2 Tb: 37 cal, 2.5 g fat (0 g sat.), 3 g carb (1 g fiber)

Did you know ...

Baking soda is a great deodorizer. Use it on cutting boards to remove any strong odors: Sprinkle liberally over entire surface, then sprinkle with vinegar and let it bubble away.

Red Relish

- **3 large (or 6 small) green onions**
- **1 medium turnip**
- **1 average bunch of radishes**
- **3 drops of red food coloring** (optional)
- **1 cup white vinegar** (240 ml)
- **1 cup Splenda™ Granular** (240 ml)
- **1 Tb. ThickenThin NotStarch™** (15 ml)
- **1 Tb. black pepper** (15 ml)
- **2 Tb. dry parsley** (30 ml)

Mince white top portions of the green onions in a food processor, pulsing on and off until fine but not pureed. Scrape onions into a large bowl. Slice the green crisp portions thinly by hand and add to bowl. Peel turnip and chop into 8 pieces. Mince in food processor until fine and add to onions in bowl. (If you have a few large pieces left but the rest looks good, stop. Remove the big portions and discard, then use the rest – you want a fine end result without hours of work, not mush!) Clean radishes (this is a great way to use up the "ugly" ones from the garden that are otherwise fine but which never seem to get eaten at my house). You guessed it! Mince and add to bowl. Measure vinegar, Splenda™, food coloring, ThickenThin™, parsley, and black pepper into processor and pulse briefly until mixed well and thickened slightly. Mix all ingredients well, and refrigerate.

Excellent with brats, hot dogs, burgers, or over salads or fish or almost anything! Fresh minced jalapeno or habanera peppers would be a great addition to this relish, if spicy is to your liking. Also good when made with all turnips and no radishes.

Yield approx. 2½ cups

Per 2 Tb: 11 cal, 0.1 g fat (0 g sat.), 2 g carb (1 g fiber)

Seafood Sauce

- ½ **cup mayonnaise** (120 ml)
- **1 Tb. grated horseradish** (15 ml)
- **2 Tb.** *TLC Catsup* (30 ml - see page 39)
- **2 tsp. lemon juice** (10 ml)

Whisk ingredients together until well mixed and smooth. *Per 2 Tb: 191 cal, 19 g fat (2 g sat.), 0 g carb*

Strawberry Jam

- **16 oz. frozen strawberries** (3 cups, 720 ml, 450 gm)
- **1 small pkg. unsweetened Kool-Aid**™ (any flavor you like that would complement)
- **4 Tb. unsweetened plain gelatin** (30 ml)
- **1 Tb. lemon juice** (15 ml)
- **1½ cups SF strawberry syrup** (360 ml)

Put berries and lemon juice in a large stockpot over medium heat. When berries have thawed sufficiently, crush. Continue to heat berries until completely soft. Mix syrup and gelatin powder and add to berries. Bring to a full rolling boil, stirring constantly. (A rolling boil is one that does not slow or stop when stirred vigorously.) Continue to boil for exactly one minute; remove from heat. Allow to cool for another minute, then skim off foam from surface. (Save this for the chef's sample, there is nothing wrong with this so far as taste goes, it just looks funny if you leave it in the jelly.) Pour the jam into glass jars or plastic containers, wipe rims, close lids, and refrigerate.

Use within 4 weeks, or freeze if longer storage is required. You can easily vary this recipe to make any flavor of fruit jam. If you like a looser consistency, reduce the amount of gelatin used.

Yield: 3 cups

Per 2 Tb: 14 cal, 0.1 g fat (0 g sat.), 1 g carb, 2 g protein

Tartar Sauce

- **¾ cup mayonnaise** (180 ml)
- **2 Tb. white vinegar** (30 ml)
- **3 Tb. Splenda™ Granular** (45 ml)
- **2 Tb. dill relish** (30 ml)

Whisk all ingredients together until well mixed and smooth.

Per 2 Tb: 135 cal, 14.5 g fat (2g sat.) 0 carbs or protein

Teriyaki Marinade & Dipping Sauce

- **¼ cup soy sauce** (60 ml)
- **¼ cup rice wine vinegar** (60 ml – be sure you do not use "seasoned" rice wine vinegar!)
- **¼ cup water** (60 ml)
- **½ tsp. minced garlic** (2.5 ml)
- **1 tsp. black pepper** (5 ml)
- **1 tsp. ThickenThin Not Starch™**
- **3 Tb. low carb jelly** (45 ml - *TLC Mixed Fruit Jelly* is perfect!)

Whisk soy sauce, vinegar, garlic, pepper, and jelly together. Blend NotStarch with water and add to contents of bowl. Sauce will thicken after standing a few minutes.

Per 2 Tb : 10 cal, 0 g fat, <1 g carb, 1.5 g protein

Seasoned Vinegar

- **8 cups white vinegar** (2 liters)
- **Garlic: 8 peeled whole cloves or 1 Tb. minced, prepared** (15 ml)
- **2 Tb. dried rosemary** (30 ml)
- **2 Tb. dried tarragon** (30 ml)
- **2 Tb. mustard seed** (30 ml)
- **2 Tb. celery seed** (30 ml)
- **2 Tb. dried thyme** (30 ml)
- **2 Tb. whole black peppercorns** (30 ml)
- **2 Tb. dry onion flakes** (30 ml)

Place all ingredients in a large glass jar. Cover and allow to steep, out of direct light, for one full month. Strain through a sieve and discard all solids. Delicious over vegetables, in salad dressings, soups, etc. I often add handfuls of fresh herbs in place of the dried. You could also add dried hot whole peppers for extra kick.

Per 2 Tb: 2 cal, 0 g fat, 0 g carb, 0 protein

Did you know ...

Plain white vinegar mixed with salt makes an excellent all-purpose cleaner. Cleans copper, bronze, brass, dishes, pots, pans, skillets, glasses, and windows. Just be sure to rinse very well.

Vinaigrette Dressings

- **½ cup** *TLC Seasoned Vinegar** (120 ml - pg. 49)
- **1 cup oil** (240 ml)
- **¼ cup water** (60 ml)
- **2 Tb. Splenda™ Granular** (30 ml)
- **½ tsp. salt** (2.5 ml)

Add oil to remaining ingredients slowly, in a thin stream, whisking or blending vigorously all the while. Shake well each time before serving.
Per 2 Tb: 122 cal, 13.5 g fat (1 g sat.), 0 g carb

Mustard: Add 1 Tb. of any flavor mustard.

Raspberry: Substitute plain white vinegar for the seasoned vinegar. Add 1 Tb. SF raspberry syrup and ½ tsp. black pepper.

Garlic Pepper: Add 2 tsp. minced garlic and 1 Tb. black pepper.

Sweet and Sour: Add 2 Tb. soy sauce, 1 Tb. black pepper, and 1 Tb. TLC mixed fruit jelly

Sweet Hot: Mix equal amounts of *TLC Jalapeno Mustard* with white vinegar and add Splenda at the rate of 2 Tb. per cup, or to taste.

If you don't wish to make or buy seasoned vinegar, white, unseasoned rice wine, or red wine vinegars are all very good in its place.

Main Dishes & Soups

Beef Stew

- **1 lb. boneless beef, diced** (450 gm)
- **3 Tb. oil** (45 ml)
- **¼ cup chopped onion** (60 ml)
- **2 Tb. seasoned or white vinegar** (30 ml)
- **1 turnip** (average size, 3.5 oz. 100 ml)
- **2 cups green beans** (480 ml)
- **1 tsp. garlic powder** (5 ml)
- **1 tsp. onion powder** (5 ml)
- **2 beef bullion cubes**
- **10 cups water** (2400 ml)
- **2 Tb. ThickenThin NotStarch™** (30 ml)

Heat oil in large stockpot over high heat until smoking hot. Add diced meat carefully, taking care not to crowd the pan. I add about half of the meat first, and wait till it all comes up to temp before adding the rest. If you throw it all in at once and lower the temperature of the pan too much, it will release all its natural juices and just sit there boiling, instead of browning in the oil and searing in the natural juices. (This technique applies to any meat you wish to sear. High heat and an uncrowded pan are your friends for the first few minutes!) Chop green beans into smaller pieces. When the meat is well browned all over, add onion and cook till transparent. Add the Notstarch™ to the vinegar and blend, then add that mixture and all the remaining ingredients to the pan at the same time. Simmer over medium low heat for an hour or more, until meat is very tender. You can also put the ingredients in a crock-pot or slow cooker at this point and leave it for the day. You can make this soup without the thickener, or you can substitute cornstarch and adjust the carb count accordingly.

6 servings, about 1.5 cups each after some evaporation. Each serving: 300 cal, 20 g fat (5 g sat.), 7 g carb (2 g fiber), 22 g protein

Beef Stroganoff

- **16 oz. sliced beef strips** (450 gm - or you could use chicken tenderloins)
- **2 Tb. oil** (30 ml)
- **½ a small onion, vertically sliced** (about 3.5 oz or 100 gm)
- **¾ cup water** (180 ml)
- **2 Tb. seasoned or red wine vinegar** (30 ml)
- **½ tsp. garlic powder** (2.5 ml)
- **1 tsp. salt** (5 ml)
- **1 tsp. black pepper** (5 ml)
- **1 cup sour cream** (240 ml)
- **1 Tb. ThickenThin NotStarch™** (15 ml)

Heat oil until smoking hot. Add meat strips, browning very well on all sides. Reduce heat, add onion, and cook and stir until onion is soft and transparent (not brown). Add vinegar and cook for 30 seconds, then add water and seasonings. Simmer, covered, until meat is tender - thirty minutes or several hours, depending on cut of meat. Five minutes before serving, stir NotStarch™ into sour cream. Add three large spoonfuls of the broth to the cream mixture, one spoonful at a time. When cream mixture is diluted and warmed from the broth you stirred in (tempered), you can add it to the pan without it curdling. Heat through, but not boil.

Delicious by itself, or over cabbage noodles or steamed vegetables.

4 servings, each: 408 cal, 28 g fat (13 g sat.), 7 g carb (2 gm fiber), 31 g protein

Chinese Chicken

- **3 cups chicken stock** (720 ml)
- **¼ cup soy sauce** (60 ml)
- **2 tsp. Splenda™ Granular** (10 ml)
- **2½ Tb. ThickenThin NotStarch™** (37.5 ml)
- **¼ cup unsalted butter, divided** (60 ml)
- **2 lb. boneless chicken breasts** (900 gm)
- **8 oz. can bamboo shoots, drained** (225 gm)
- **7 oz. sliced celery** (200 gm, 2 cups or 480 ml)
- **5 oz. fresh slivered green beans** (1.5 cups, 360 ml)
- **1 cup walnuts** (240 ml)
- **Ground ginger**

Whisk together chicken stock, soy sauce, Splenda™ and NotStarch™, to allow liquid to set and to begin to thicken while you proceed with the rest. Sliver fresh green beans at least in half, and quarter any larger beans. (You could use canned beans, but I would either stick with fresh, or substitute bean sprouts.) Slice celery ribs about ¼ inch thick, crossways. Trim chicken and chop into bite size pieces. Season with salt and pepper. Place walnuts and 1 Tb. of butter in a microwave proof bowl, and cover tightly with plastic wrap. Stab twice with a knife to make vents and microwave for two to three minutes, until butter disappears; sprinkle with ginger and set aside. Melt remaining butter in large sauté pan and add chicken slowly, so as not to lower the pan temperature too quickly. When chicken is golden, add vegetables and bamboo shoots and sauté additional minute or two. Add liquid and simmer for about five minutes, until liquid is thickened and beans are tender-crisp. Serve alone or over cabbage noodles or low carb pasta. Sprinkle walnuts over the top of each serving.

Yield: 6 servings, each: 396 cal, 22 g fat (6 g sat.), 8 g carb (4 g fiber), 42 g protein

Chicken Alfredo

- **24 oz. boneless skinless chicken breasts** (675 gm)
- **2 Tb. olive oil** (30 ml)
- **2 tsp. garlic powder** (10 ml)
- **1/3 cup heavy cream** (80 ml)
- **1/4 cup unsalted butter** (60 ml)
- **1/3 cup grated Parmesan cheese** (80 ml)

**Cut chicken into strips and sauté in hot olive oil until browned and almost cooked through.
Add remaining ingredients to pan and heat and stir until it reaches the proper consistency. Do not allow to boil or it may separate.**

Serve over a bed of cabbage or egg noodles, mashed faux-tatoes, steamed green beans, or by itself.

4 servings, each: 458 cal, 33 g fat (15 sat.), 1 g carb, 39 g protein

---

Did you know ...

You can make a good substitute for sour cream by blending together 1 cup cottage cheese (240 ml)**, 1/4 cup cream** (60 ml) **and 1 tsp. of vinegar** (5 ml).

Chicken Broccoli Strata

- **¼ cup unsalted butter** (60 ml)
- **4 Tb. ThickenThin NotStarch™** (60 ml)
- **½ tsp. salt** (2.5 ml)
- **1 cup heavy whipping cream** (240 ml)
- **1 cup water** (240 ml)
- **½ cup grated Parmesan cheese** (120 ml)
- **1 lb. cooked broccoli, fresh or frozen** (450 ml)
- **½ oz. crushed pork rinds** (about ¼ cup, 60 ml)
- **1.5 lbs. cooked chicken, deboned** (450 gm)

Melt butter in saucepan. Stir in thickener and cook for one minute. Add water and cream all at once and whisk until smooth and thickened and bubbly. Add Parmesan cheese and remove from heat.
Scatter cooked broccoli and chicken pieces evenly in a greased casserole dish. Pour sauce over all, then sprinkle crushed pork rinds on the top.
Bake at 350 degrees F (180 C) for 45-60 minutes, until the top is a deep golden brown.

I used skinned, stewed chicken thighs but you could substitute any leftover meat or fish with good results.

6 servings, each: 577 cal, 40 g fat (19 g sat.), 9 g carb (3 g fiber), 45 g protein

---

Did you know ...

When stewing chicken, leave the chicken in the water to cool after cooking, and it will have a lot more flavor. (Use common sense here - refrigerate when wise!)

Chicken Parmesan

- **boneless skinless chicken breasts** (large ones are best, about 24 oz or 675 gm total)
- **Canned, diced tomatoes, drained** (28 oz., 750 ml)
- **1 sweet red bell pepper, diced** (about a cup, 120 ml, 100 gm)
- **¼ cup chopped onion** (60 ml)
- **1 tsp. minced garlic** (5 ml,, or add more to taste)
- **5 Tb. olive oil, divided** (75 ml)
- **1 Tb. Italian seasoning** (15 ml)
- **2 Tb. red wine vinegar** (30 ml)
- **2 Tb. Splenda™ Granular** (30 ml)
- **½ cup grated Parmesan cheese** (120 ml)
- **½ cup shredded mozzarella cheese** (120 ml)

Put half the olive oil into an already hot pan. Add chopped red pepper and cook for one minute. Add chopped onion and minced garlic and cook one more minute. Add Italian seasoning, lightly drained tomatoes, salt and pepper to taste, Splenda™, and vinegar. Reduce heat to low, cover, and simmer. Meanwhile, preheat oven to 375 degrees F (190 C). Season chicken with salt and pepper. Place one piece between two pieces of plastic wrap and pound with a heavy object like a wine bottle or meat mallet. Work from the inside out. Don't over do it, just try to make the fat side about even to the thin side. Repeat with all breasts. Put remaining olive oil into another HOT pan over high heat. Sear the chicken breasts quickly (high heat, remember) until well browned. Put a little of the hot sauce in the bottom of a casserole dish. Arrange the chicken breasts evenly over the sauce layer. Carefully pour sauce over all. Sprinkle with Parmesan cheese. Top that with mozzarella cheese. Bake for about 40 minutes, until cheese is golden brown and chicken is thoroughly cooked.

4 servings, each: 493 cal, 29 g fat (7 g sat.), 9 g carb (2 g fiber), 46 g protein

Clam Chowder

- ¼ cup chopped onion (60 ml)
- 1 Tb. butter (15 ml)
- 1 Tb. olive oil (15 ml)
- 1 cup bottled clam juice (240 ml)
- 1½ cups water (360 ml)
- 1 cup heavy whipping cream (240 ml)
- 1 tsp. Old Bay™ seasoning (5 ml)
- ½ tsp. black pepper (2.5 ml)
- 1 cup chopped canned clams with juice (240 ml)

Sauté onions in butter and olive oil in saucepan over medium heat until soft. Do not allow onions to turn brown. Add remaining ingredients and heat through. Do not boil. Serve immediately.

2 servings, each: 566 cal, 57 g fat (31 g sat.), 4 carbs, 3 g protein

---

Did you know ...

You should never use a toxic cleaner inside your microwave. The fumes it can create the next time you cook food in it can be harmful - and can even transfer to your food!

Instead, make a general non-toxic cleaning solution with 4 Tb. baking soda or vinegar to 1 qt. water. Boil this mixture inside of the oven for two minutes to loosen baked on foods, then wipe down thoroughly. You can then use the warm solution to clean other surfaces. This is an economical and safe way to clean your kitchen!

Corn Dogs

- **Low carb hot dogs**
- **Eggs**
- *TLC Bake Mix*
- **Water**
- **Sticks**
- **A mild flavored oil for frying - like grapeseed**

Mix breading batter as follows: 1 egg to each ¼ cup (60 ml) **of bake mix. How much you mix will depend on how much you plan to make, but 2 eggs and ½ cup** (120 ml) **bake mix works for 6 of my dogs.**

Add 1 tsp. water (5 ml) **to egg and bake mix, then add additional water 1 tsp.** (5 ml) **at a time until batter reaches the proper consistency, so that when you dip a hot dog in it, it coats the outside thoroughly without being too thick. Depending on the humidity in your area, you may need to add a little more or less water to get it just right.**

Drive a stick into the end of each dog and dip and roll in batter. Hold above bowl and allow excess batter to run off, then deep fry in hot oil until golden brown and hot dog is heated through, about three to four minutes.

Drain on paper towels and serve piping hot. It's hard to tell these from the originals, especially with some *TLC Catsup* **to dip them in!**

When made with 0 carb dogs & **ULC** *or* **SF** *Bake Mix, 207 cal, 16 g fat (5g sat.), 2 g carb, 13 g protein, each.* **MC** *Bake Mix: 3 g carb each*

Crab or Lobster Bisque

- **½ cup chopped onion** (1.5 oz., or 40 gm, 120 ml)
- **¼ cup thinly sliced celery** (2 oz. or 60 gm/ml)
- **2 Tb. butter** (30 ml)
- **2 Tb. dry white wine** (30 ml – optional but highly recommended.)
- **1 cup fish or chicken stock** (240 ml)
- **2 cups water** (480 ml)
- **1 cup heavy whipping cream** (240 ml)
- **1 tsp. Old Bay™ seasoning** (5 ml)
- **2 tsp. dried tarragon** (10 ml)
- **1 Tb. ThickenThin NotStarch™** (optional – 15 ml)
- **1 tsp. salt** (5 ml)
- **½ tsp. black pepper** (10 ml)
- **1 cup cooked crab or lobster meat** (240 ml, canned crab is fine)

Sauté onions and celery in butter in saucepan over medium heat until soft. Do not allow vegetables to turn brown. Add wine and cook for one minute, then add remaining ingredients and stir gently over medium low heat until warmed through. Do not allow soup to boil.

Serve immediately. This is quick and easy to prepare, yet rich and elegant on the palate.

4 servings, each: 368 cal, 34 g fat (20 g sat.), 4 g carb (1 g fiber), 10 g protein

Cream of Vegetable Soup

- **4 cups chopped low carb vegetables of your choice** (1 liter - I suggest cauliflower, broccoli, celery, asparagus, or mushrooms.)
- **4 cups of canned chicken stock** (1 liter)
- **1 cup of heavy cream** (240 ml)
- **½ cup butter** (120 ml)
- **1 cup water** (240 ml)
- **3 Tb. ThickenThin NotStarch™** (45 ml)
- **1 Tb. garlic powder** (15 ml)
- **1 tsp. salt** (5 ml)
- **1 Tb. black pepper** (5 ml)
- **2 tsp. marjoram** (10 ml)
- **1 Tb. onion powder** (15 ml)
- **Dash hot pepper sauce, optional, to taste**

Prepare vegetables as needed (Peel the broccoli stalks and slice thinly. Chop florets of broccoli or cauliflower roughly. Slice mushrooms or celery, etc.) Boil the vegetables in the chicken stock till tender.

Reserve 1/3 of the vegetables. Puree the remainder in batches in the blender and return to pan along with reserved vegetables.

Melt butter in another pan. Mix the NotStarch™ with water till dissolved. Add to butter and heat till thickened. Stir in the heavy cream, and add the warm cream mixture to the pureed vegetable mixture. Heat through, but be careful not to boil!

6 generous servings, carbs vary depending on vegetables used. Made with broccoli, each serving has 339 cal, 31 g fat (18 g sat.), 11 carbs (5 grams fiber), 8 g protein.

Cheese is a great addition! How 'bout bacon?

Creamy Seafood Bake

- **1-2 lbs. cod, orange roughy, haddock or other mild white fish** (500 – 900 gm)
- **12 scallops**
- **5 Tb. olive oil** (75 ml)
- **1 cup sour cream** (240 ml)
- **2 Tb. garlic powder** (30 ml)
- **2 Tb. chopped fresh herbs** (30 ml - I used garlic chives but dill weed, thyme, or rosemary would be lovely too)
- **2 tsp. salt** (10 ml)
- **2 tsp. fresh ground black pepper** (10 ml)

Preheat oven to 425 degrees F (220 C). Rinse fish and scallops and pat dry. Pour olive oil on a plate. Roll fish fillets and scallops in the oil and then salt and pepper both sides of each one. Arrange oiled portions in one layer in a baking pan. Sprinkle tops with garlic powder and then cover with sour cream and chopped herbs. Bake approximately 10-12 minutes, until fish flakes easily with fork and scallops are tender.

Even the kid who "hates fish" ate this meal....

Made with 24 oz. of cod, 4 generous servings, each: 452 cal, 30 g fat (9 g sat.), 7 g carb, 37 g protein

---

Did you know ...

To help prevent eggshells from cracking, add a pinch of salt to the water before hard-boiling.

Croquettes

These are a bit more trouble than your average crab cakes, but I think you'll find the extra effort is justified. And they freeze beautifully for later use, so make a bunch and freeze them in small packages. Just heat them in the microwave and you've got a great low carb snack or entrée in seconds. This is my favorite way to deal with leftovers that I am sick of in their original form. I occasionally cook large pieces of meat just for this purpose.

Beginning Fry Cooks refer to *Deep Frying TLC*, page 14.

- **3 cups cooked meat, fish or poultry, chopped** (720 ml)
- **½ tsp. salt** (2.5 ml)
- **cayenne pepper to taste**
- **2 Tb. onion, grated** (30 ml)
- **1 tsp. lemon juice** (5 ml)
- **1 tsp. celery leaves, finely chopped** (5 ml)*
- **2 tsp. minced parsley** (10 ml)*
- **1 cup heavy cream** (240 ml)
- **3 Tb. unsalted butter** (45 ml)
- **1½ Tb. ThickenThin NotStarch™** (23 ml)
- **1½ cups pork rind crumbs** (360 ml)
- **4 eggs -- beaten**
- **oil for frying**

*You can substitute 1 tsp. (5 ml) dried parsley for both the celery leaves and the fresh parsley.

Mix the meat or fish with the salt, cayenne pepper to taste (start with ½ tsp. or 2.5 ml, and if you like spicy foods, double that), the grated onion, lemon juice, chopped celery leaves, and parsley.

Melt butter in a saucepan. Add the starch and cook over medium heat one minute, stirring constantly.

(recipe continued next page)

Add cream all at once and whisk over heat until smooth and thick. Remove from heat and allow to cool for ten minutes.

Add the sauce to the meat mixture, along with 2 beaten eggs, and mix well before spreading out on a platter to cool thoroughly and become firm (you may refrigerate or freeze the mixture at this point to chill it, but don't let it form ice crystals).

Beat the two remaining eggs in a small bowl. Place the pork rind crumbs in another bowl. Wet your hands to reduce the mixture sticking to them. I often spritz them with my Misto™ oil mister as well. Spoon out 1 heaping tablespoon of the mixture and form each croquette into an egg-sized oval shape with your hands.

Dip each croquette in the beaten eggs, and then roll in crushed pork rinds, wheat bran, or Parmesan cheese. But I <u>highly</u> recommend the pork rinds instead. The cheese tends to burn before the insides are done, the bran adds carbs, and you would NEVER ever guess from the finished product that the pork rind crumbs are in fact, pork rinds, and not breadcrumbs.

Fry in deep hot fat for 1-2 minutes, a few at a time, depending on size. Drain briefly on paper towels and serve immediately.

Serve with dipping sauces. These freeze beautifully for later use.

Made with chicken, 16 servings, each: 218 cal, 18 g fat (6 g sat.), 1 g carb, 13 g protein

Egg Drop Soup

- **1 bunch green onions, sliced** (¼ cup, 1 oz, 30 gm)
- **1 Tb. oil** (15 ml)
- **5 cups chicken stock** (1200 ml)
- **1 Tb. ThickenThin NotStarch™** (15 ml)
- **2 Tb. soy sauce** (30 ml)
- **1 tsp. Chinese 5 spice powder** (5 ml - optional)
- **2 beaten eggs**

Cook onion in oil in large stockpot over medium heat until translucent. Add chicken stock, soy sauce, and 5-spice powder. Remove a small amount of liquid, mix with NotStarch until smooth, and then return mixture to stockpot. Boil for several minutes, until slightly thickened. Drizzle beaten eggs into soup, stirring constantly.

4 srv, each: 111 cal, 6 g fat (1 g sat.), 2 carbs (1 gm fiber), 11 g protein

Fish Fritters

- **16 oz. cooked cooled flaked fish** (450 gm – even canned tuna or salmon, would do nicely)
- **2 Tb. oil** (30 ml)
- **1 cup** *TLC Bake Mix* (240 ml)
- **3 eggs**
- **1 tsp. salt** (5 ml)
- **1 tsp. pepper** (5 ml)
- **¼ cup grated Parmesan cheese** (60 ml)
- **Oil for frying**

Mix fish with bake mix, Parmesan, and salt and pepper. Beat eggs slightly, then add to bowl. Mixture should be sticky, and easily form a ball. Scoop out into uniform sized balls, using an oiled ice cream scoop or two spoons. Deep fry a few at a time in hot oil until golden brown and hot all the way through. Drain on paper towels and serve with assorted dipping sauces.

12 servings, each: 171 cal, 11 g fat (1 g sat.), 2 g carb, 15 g protein

Festive Fajita Salad

- **Romaine lettuce**
- **Onion and bell pepper strips (add jalapeno strips if you like HOT)**
- **Steak or chicken strips**
- **Hot Pepper sauce**
- **Shredded cheddar, jack, or pepper jack cheese**
- **Picante Sauce or a commercial unsweetened salsa**
- **Sour Cream**
- **Toasted low carb tortilla strips (optional)**

Sauté onions and peppers with meat until veggies are tender-crisp and meat is cooked through.

Add several tablespoons (to taste) of hot pepper sauce to the pan. WARNING - Do not inhale or lean over the pan at this time! .... ooh-chi-mama, the fumes..... My favorite sauce is made with Scotch Bonnet peppers and 2-3 Tb. over 2 pounds of meat is plenty spicy for me.

Shake the pan gently, to burn the sauce onto the outside of the meat.

Melt cheese over the top and then slide the hot mixture right onto a bed of lettuce.

Top with a half-cup of fresh TLC Picante sauce or 1/4 cup salsa, a dollop of sour cream, and a sprinkling of toasted tortilla strips. YUM. Fast, easy, filling, and never boring. I eat this once a week. Black soy beans would be a great addition too.

Carbs and calories vary wildly, depending on quantities and ingredients used - but one meal-size salad made with 2 cups Romaine, 6 oz. chicken, 1 tsp. pepper sauce, 1/4 of a small onion, 1/2 an average bell pepper, 3 oz. cheese, 1/2 cup TLC picante, and 2 Tb. Sour cream would equal 673 calories, 42 g fat (22 g sat.), 16 g carb (5 g fiber), 60 g protein.

French Onion Soup

- **1 small onion** (about 6 oz., or 170 gm)
- **2 Tb. olive oil** (30 ml)
- **2 Tb. unsalted butter** (30 ml)
- **2 Tb.** *TLC Bake Mix* (30 ml)
- **6 cups beef stock or bullion** (1500 ml - I used 2 beef bullion cubes and 1 vegetable bullion cube plus specified amount of water).
- **4 cups water** (1 liter)
- **1 tsp. garlic powder** (5 ml)
- **1 Tb. red wine vinegar** (15 ml)
- **1 Tb. Worcestershire sauce** (15 ml)
- **½ tsp. salt** (2.5 ml)
- **1 tsp. black pepper** (5 ml)

Heat oil and butter in large stockpot over medium heat. Vertically slice (julienne) the onion, and sauté in oil/butter mixture slowly until completely browned and very crispy (caramelized). Discard any excess grease. Stir bake mix into onions and cook and stir for two minutes. Add bullion or stock to pan slowly, while stirring. The liquid should start to boil immediately upon hitting the hot surface of the pan, de-glazing it for you and making the stock very dark and rich. Stir in water, garlic powder, vinegar, salt, pepper, and Worcestershire sauce, and simmer, covered, for 15-30 minutes.

6 servings, each: 110 cal, 9 g fat (3 g sat.), 4 g carb, 2 g protein

Optional: Float one round melba toast on the surface of individual bowls of soup. Cover with Swiss cheese, and put under broiler until cheese bubbles and browns. You may double or triple the amount of onions if you can afford the additional carbs.

Green Chili

- **1 lb. boneless pork, diced** (450 gm)
- **2 Tb. oil** (30 ml)
- **7 roasted green chilies, diced** (you can use canned, or you can roast your own, fresh)
- **4 cups water** (1 liter - I use all the liquid drained from the whole canned chili's, and then add water as needed)
- **2 cups chicken stock** (480 ml)
- **2 tsp. ground cumin** (10 ml)
- **2 Tb. vinegar** (30 ml)
- **3 Tb. hot "wing" sauce** (45 ml)
- **2 Tb. ThickenThin NotStarch™** (30 ml)
- **1 tsp. salt** (5 ml)
- **1 Tb. black pepper** (15 ml)

Heat oil in large stockpot over high heat until smoking hot. Add diced meat carefully, taking care not to crowd the pan. When the meat is well browned all over, add the Notstarch™ to the vinegar and blend, then add that mixture and the remaining ingredients to the pan. Simmer over medium low heat for about an hour, until meat is very tender.

You can make this soup without the thickener, or you can substitute cornstarch and adjust the carb count accordingly.

6 servings, each: 296 cal, 19.5 g fat (5 g sat.), 5 g carb (2 g fiber), 22 g protein

My children love this soup. You could always add some jalapenos in place of some of the green chilies, if you like things spicier.

Hot and Sour Soup

- **1 lb. boneless pork, diced** (450 gm)
- **2 Tb. oil** (30 ml)
- **3 cups chicken stock** (720 ml)
- **5 cups water** (1200 ml)
- **¼ cup soy sauce** (60 ml)
- **¼ cup vinegar** (60 ml - I use rice wine vinegar – make sure it does NOT say "seasoned", a euphemism in this case for "sweetened!"
- **1 tsp. black pepper** (5 ml)
- **1 Tb. ThickenThin NotStarch™** (15 ml)
- **1 cup bamboo shoots** (240 ml)

Heat oil in large stockpot over high heat until smoking hot. Add diced meat carefully, taking care not to crowd the pan. When the meat is well browned all over, add the chicken stock and water. Add the Notstarch™ to the soy sauce and blend, then add that mixture and the remaining ingredients to the pan. Simmer over medium low heat for about an hour, until meat is very tender.

You can make this soup without the thickener, or you can substitute cornstarch and adjust the carb count accordingly.

6 servings, each: 262 cal, 17 g fat (4 g sat.), 2 g carb (1 g fiber), 24 g protein

---

Did you know ...

You can check the freshness of eggs by putting them in a bowl of salted water. If they sink, they are fresh. If they come back up to the surface, throw them out!

Impossible Breakfast Pie

- **10 oz. frozen spinach, thawed** (280 ml)
- **8 slices cooked bacon, crumbled**
- **1 cup sour cream** (240 ml)
- **1 cup cottage cheese** (240 ml)
- **½ cup** *TLC Bake Mix* (120 ml)
- **¼ cup melted butter** (60 ml)
- **2 eggs**
- **1 tomato**
- **¼ cup grated Parmesan** (60 ml)

Preheat oven to 350 degrees F (180 C). Grease pie plate. Squeeze all water out of spinach, then separate and scatter in the bottom of the pie pan. Cover with layer of crumbled bacon. Mix sour cream, cottage cheese, butter, bake mix, and eggs. Pour into pie plate. Slice tomato very thin and lay on top. Sprinkle with Parmesan. Bake for 35 minutes, until golden brown. Filling should be soft, but not watery.

8 servings, each: 374 cal, 30 g fat (8 g sat.), 6 g carb (1 g fiber), 19 g protein - When using MC Bake Mix: + 1 g carb

Mexicali Quiche

Substitute 1 lb. (450 gm) **cooked drained chorizo sausage and 2 cups** (480 ml) **shredded pepper jack cheese for spinach and bacon. Omit melted butter. Sprinkle 1 Tb.** (15 ml) **chopped black olives over top instead of the Parmesan cheese and tomato. Bake as directed otherwise.**

8 servings, each: 474 cal, 37.5 g fat (16 g sat.), 5 g carb, 27 g protein

Lemon Chicken

- **¼ cup olive oil** (60 ml)
- **1½ lbs. raw chicken pieces** (I used boneless skinless breasts, about 700 gm)
- **1 Tb. lemon zest** (15 ml)
- **¼ cup fresh squeezed lemon juice** (60 ml)
- **¼ cup chopped green onions** (60 ml)
- **¼ cup heavy cream** (60 ml)
- **¼ cup water** (60 ml)
- **2 Tb. sour cream** (30 ml)

Season chicken with salt and black pepper. Heat pan to a high temperature, then add oil and chicken pieces (do not overcrowd pan). Sauté until all pieces are well browned on all sides. Drain and discard any excess grease.

Reduce heat to medium, add onion and lemon zest, and cook for one more minute. Mix lemon juice with water, cream, and sour cream, and add to pan. Continue to heat over medium heat, stirring often, until the chicken is cooked through and the sauce is the proper consistency, about ten minutes for boneless breasts, longer if you use larger pieces with bones.

Delicious over a bed of cabbage noodles or low carb pasta, or all by itself.

4 servings, each: 342 cal, 19 g fat (6 sat.), 5 g carb (1 g fiber), 37 g protein

Meatloaf

- **1½ lbs. ground beef, elk, venison, pork sausage or a combination thereof** (675 gm - I like to mix ground beef and pork or Italian sausage in equal amounts.)
- **1 cup wheat bran** (240 ml - you could substitute part ground flax seeds also)
- **½ cup boiling water** (120 ml)
- **1 beef bullion cube**
- **2 Tb. dried onion flakes** (30 ml)
- **1 Tb. dry parsley** (15 ml)
- **1 tsp. black pepper** (5 ml)
- **1 Tb. garlic powder** (15 ml)
- **3 Tb. tomato paste** (45 ml)
- **½ cup shredded cheddar cheese** (120 ml)
- **2 eggs**

Preheat oven to 375 degrees F (190 C). Pour boiling water over wheat bran, onion flakes, and bullion and allow to soften for ten minutes. Add spices, and tomato paste, and mix well. Add bran mixture to cold meat, shredded cheese, and eggs, and mix well. Form into two loaves and bake for one hour fifteen minutes.

12 servings, each: 239 cal, 20 g fat (7 sat.), 5 g carb (2 g fiber), 10 g protein

OPTIONAL: Divide 2 or more Tb. (30+ ml) *TLC Barbecue Sauce or Catsup* **over tops of loaves halfway through baking time.**

Meaty Red Chili

- **1 lb. chorizo or other sausage** (450 gm)
- **1 lb. chuck or other steak, diced** (450 gm)
- **8 cups water** (2 liters)
- **1 Tb. tomato paste** (15 ml)
- **1¾ cups diced canned tomatoes, with juices** (14.5 oz, 406 gm, 420 ml)
- **2 tsp. diced jalapeno peppers** (10 ml)
- **2 cups black soy beans** (480 ml)
- **2 tsp. ground cumin seed** (10 ml)
- **1 tsp. garlic powder** (5 ml)
- **1 tsp. salt** (5 ml)
- **1½ tsp. black pepper** (7.5 ml)
- **1 tsp. cayenne pepper** (5 ml, adjust to taste)
- **1 Tb. ThickenThin NotStarch™** (15 ml, optional)

Cook meats together in large stockpot, stirring, until well browned. Drain well, and return to pan, discarding grease. Add remaining ingredients, except for NotStarch™. Bring to a boil, cover and simmer for an hour or more. (You could also just place ingredients in a crock-pot or slow cooker for the day.) Before serving, remove a bit of the liquid and mix with the NotStarch™, then mix that into the rest of the chili and stir gently until slightly thickened. You can also omit the NotStarch™ entirely, and just remove the lid and allow the soup to reduce to the proper consistency, but that will yield a little less soup.

6 servings, each: 511 cal, 31 g fat (10 sat.), 11 g carb (6 g fiber), 46 g protein

Nut-Encrusted Fish

- **16 oz. cod** (450 gm - or other mild white fish such as orange roughy, or sea bass)
- **½ cup nut meal or finely chopped nuts** (120 ml - I prefer and analyzed almonds)
- **1 egg, beaten**
- **2 Tb. soy flour** (30 ml - can use other flours)
- **1 tsp. sea salt** (5 ml)
- **1 Tb. minced dried parsley** (15 ml)
- **1 tsp. fresh ground black pepper** (5 ml)
- **2 Tb. olive oil** (30 ml)

Preheat oven to 375 degrees F (180 C). Cut fish into serving size pieces, if necessary. Mix spices with flour and dredge fish through mixture. Dip each coated piece of fish first into the beaten egg, then into the chopped almonds, until encrusted with nuts on all sides. Heat olive oil in oven-proof skillet (I prefer cast iron) until almost smoking (hot!), brown fish quickly on one side, then turn over. Take great care while turning each piece over not to dislodge the nut coating. Place pan in hot oven for about 20 minutes, until fish is milky white all the way through and flakes easily with fork.

4 servings, each: 351 cal, 24 g fat (2 sat.), 8 g carb (4 g fiber), 27 g protein

---

Did you know ...

Fabric softener sheets will ...

**Freshen the air in your home? Place an individual fabric softener sheet in a drawer or hang one in the closet.
Freshen the air in your car? Place a fabric softener sheet under the seat.**

Radish Greens Soup

- **3 Tb. unsalted butter** (45 ml)
- **1/3 cup diced onion** (80 ml)
- **2 bunches radish greens, cleaned** (about 2 cups or 480 ml)
- **1 large turnip, peeled and diced** (about 1 cup, 240 ml)
- **4 cups chicken stock** (1 liter)
- **2 cups water** (480 ml)
- **1 cup heavy cream** (240 ml)
- **1 tsp. salt** (5 ml)
- **1 tsp. black pepper** (5 ml)
- **1 tsp. garlic powder** (5 ml)
- **1 tsp. ground thyme** (5 ml)

In a medium stockpot, melt butter over medium heat. Stir in onions, and sauté until transparent. Add radish greens, and cook until wilted, about 4 minutes. Add turnips, chicken stock, and water and cook, stirring occasionally, until turnips are tender. Force the mixture through a food mill or sieve into a medium bowl (this is easiest to do in several smaller batches). Stir in the heavy cream, and season with salt, pepper and thyme. Strain the puréed mixture again through a fine mesh sieve into the original pot. Bring soup just to a simmer over medium heat. Serve garnished with radish zest, if desired.

4 servings, each: 255 cal, 22 g fat (13 sat.), 7 g carb (1 g fiber), 8 g protein, **,** *assuming that radish greens are equivalent to turnip greens - I could not locate a reliable count).*

You could substitute other greens, of course, whatever you have available or ready in the garden. You can also mix several different kinds of greens.

Santa Fe Chicken

- **8 boneless skinless chicken breast portions,** (approx. 4 oz. or 115 gm. each)
- **8 whole roasted green chilies**
- **4 oz. pepper jack cheese, sliced** (225 gm)
- **2 Tb. unsalted butter** (30 ml)
- **1 Tb.** *TLC Chili Paste* **or Red Thai Curry Paste** (15 ml)
- **¼ cup shredded cheddar cheese** (1 oz. 30 gm, 60 ml)
- **¼ cup shredded pepper jack cheese** (1 oz. 30 gm, 60 ml)
- **¼ cup heavy cream** (60 ml)
- **¼ cup water** (60 ml)
- **1 Tb. ThickenThin NotStarch™** (15 ml)
- **Crumbled bacon and sautéed sliced mushrooms for garnish, optional**

Place chicken breasts between layers of plastic wrap, one at a time, and pound with meat mallet or bottom of heavy glass bottle until flattened and of equal thickness. They do not need to be paper-thin, do not overdo it - just try to make the fat side as thin as the rest. Place peppers and sliced pepper jack cheese atop chicken pieces. Roll edges over, to secure contents inside. Place seam side down in greased loaf pan, sides touching. Bake in 350 degree F (180 C) oven, uncovered, for about an hour, until tops are well browned. Ten minutes before serving, make sauce by mixing NotStarch™ with water in a small saucepan. Add butter and cream and heat until thickened and bubbly. Stir in chili paste and cheeses and continue to heat, stirring constantly, until cheese is melted and sauce is smooth. Serve sauce over tops of chicken pieces. Garnish with bacon and mushrooms, if desired.

8 servings, each: 256 cal, 15 g fat (7 sat.), 2 g carb, 28 g protein

Sausage Gravy

- **1 lb. pork sausage** (450 gm)
- **3 Tb.** *TLC Bake Mix* (45 ml)
- **1 Tb. ThickenThin NotStarch™** (15 ml)
- **1 cup heavy cream** (240 ml)
- **½ cup water** (120 ml)
- **1 tsp. garlic powder** (5 ml)
- **1 tsp. onion powder** (5 ml)
- **2 tsp. black pepper** (10 ml)
- **½ tsp. salt** (2.5 ml)

Brown and cook crumbled sausage; drain and discard all excess grease. Whisk cream, water, bake mix, spices, and NotStarch™ together until smooth and without lumps. Add liquid ingredients to cooked sausage in pan and bring to a boil, stirring constantly, until thickened. Serve over eggs or biscuits.

6 servings, each: 426 cal, 42 g fat (35 sat.), 4 g carb (1 g fiber), 9 g protein

Smoky Beef Brisket

- **3 lb. beef brisket** (1400 gm)
- **1 Tb. onion flakes** (30 ml)
- **1/3 cup liquid smoke** (80 ml)
- **1 tsp. minced garlic** (5 ml)
- **heavy duty aluminum cooking bag**

Place brisket fat side up in cooking bag, or fashion your own out of double or triple layers of heavy-duty foil. Mix onion flakes, garlic, and liquid smoke and pour over roast. Seal cooking bag tightly, place on a baking sheet, and bake at 325 degrees F (165 C) for 2-3 hours. Scrape off fat layer and slice thinly, cross the grain.

8 servings, each: 372 cal, 17 g fat (6 sat.), 0 g carb 50 g protein

Southwestern Pizza Bake

- **4 Tb. olive oil, divided** (60 ml)
- **1½ cups Parmesan cheese** (360 ml)
- **1½ cups shredded cheddar** (360 ml)
- **8 ounces cream cheese, softened** (225 gm)
- **6 large eggs**
- **¾ cup cream** (180 ml)
- **1 Tb. cumin** (15 ml)
- **1 tsp. black pepper** (5 ml)
- **1 tsp. ground oregano** (5 ml)
- **1 tsp. garlic powder** (5 ml)
- **1 Tb. dry parsley** (15 ml)
- **1½ cups** *TLC Picante Sauce* (360 ml)
- **1 lb. boneless chicken, in strips** (450 gm)
- **2 Tb. hot pepper sauce** (30 ml)
- **2 cups grated cheese** (480 ml)

Preheat oven to 375F (180C). Beat cream cheese until smooth. Slowly add cream, then eggs, then spices, mix well; set aside. Add 2 Tb. oil to 13" x 9" dish to grease. Scatter 3 cups of cheese on the bottom of dish. Pour egg mixture over cheese and bake for 25-30 minutes, until lightly browned. Meanwhile, brown the chicken strips in remaining olive oil in a very hot pan until cooked through. Add 2 Tb. of your favorite hot sauce to the pan and shake or stir it gently so as to coat the chicken strips with the hot sauce. WARNING: Don't lean or inhale over the stove when you add the hot sauce! Remove base from oven and cover it with salsa, chicken strips, and remaining shredded cheese. Increase oven heat to 450 F, return pan to oven, and bake for an additional 10-15 minutes or so, until cheese melts, browns, and bubbles.

12 servings, each: 401 cal, 30 g fat (15 sat.), 4 g carb , 27 g protein

Make a traditionally flavored pizza by using mozzarella, 1/2 cup tomato sauce in place of salsa, and more typical pizza toppings & spices.

(You could cut this recipe in half and cook it in an 8x8 pan.)

TacoSagna

- **1½ lbs. ground beef, pork, elk, venison, sausage, chorizo, or some combination thereof** (675 gm)
- **6 Tb.** *TLC Red Ancho Chili Paste* (75 ml - or a 1.25 oz. pkg. of taco seasoning mix)
- **27 oz. can of whole green chilies** (750 ml – Drain and reserve 2 Tb. {30 ml} of the canning juice
- **15 oz. container ricotta cheese** (425 gm)
- **¼ cup sour cream** (60 ml)
- **4 oz. cream cheese** (115 gm)
- **½ cup water** (120 ml)
- **2 Tb. hot sauce – I use red Tabasco™** (30 ml)
- **4 ea. low carb tortillas or 2 med. zucchinis, sliced lengthwise**

Preheat oven to 350 degrees F (180 C). Season meat with salt and pepper. Crumble, brown, and drain off grease. Stir in chili paste (or taco seasoning mix and enough water so it mixes easily - about ¼ cup 60 ml). In a small bowl, whisk together ricotta, sour cream, cream cheese, reserved chili juice, hot sauce, and ½ cup water. Spread a little of the white sauce to cover the bottom of a 13" x 9" pan. Cover sauce with a layer of tortillas, ripped into the right shapes and overlapped slightly (or sliced zucchini or another layer of chilies). Sprinkle meat mixture evenly over base; cover with a single layer of whole green chilies and pour remaining white sauce over all. Bake 45 - 60 minutes, until top starts to brown and crack. Remove from oven and allow to stand for five minutes before serving.

12 servings, each: 327 cal, 21 g fat (10 sat.), 12 g carb (3 g fiber), 24 g protein - 13 g carb (0 g fiber) made without tortillas and using 2 cans of chilies - 305 cal, 20 g fat (10 sat.), 9 g carb (3 g fiber), 21 g protein made with zucchini in place of tortillas - ***Add one carb per serving when made with taco seasoning in place of TLC Chili Paste.***

Tuna Casserole

- **4 cups cooked chopped broccoli** (1 liter—you could always substitute other low carb vegetables)
- **24 oz. well-drained tuna** (700 gm)
- **2 cups sour cream** (480 ml)
- **½ cup heavy cream** (120 ml)
- **2½ cups shredded cheddar cheese** (600 ml)
- **8 slices cooked crumbled bacon**

Preheat oven to 400 degrees F (200 C) and grease a square 9x9 inch pan.
Layer broccoli in the bottom of the pan.
Cover broccoli with tuna.
Mix sour cream and heavy cream together and spread out evenly over contents of pan.
Next, add an even layer of shredded cheese.
Top the cheese with the bacon bits.
Bake for approximately thirty minutes.
Allow to set for five minutes before serving. (You may need to tilt pan over sink and drain any excess water that has accumulated in bottom of pan.)

9 servings, each: 529 cal, 37 g fat (18 sat.), 7 g carb (2 g fiber), 42 g protein

Did you know ...

You can make it easier to mix up unsweetened peanut butter by turning the jar upside down for 24 hours first, and allowing some of the peanut oil to flow back down through the drained mass below.

Side Dishes & Vegetables

Barbecued Beans

These are not like the barbecued beans we used to enjoy, but I couldn't think of a better name!

- **4 cups cooked green beans** (2 cans, 1 liter)
- **8 slices crumbled cooked bacon** (about 1.5 oz or 40 gm)
- **½ cup** *TLC Barbecue Sauce* (120 ml)
- **¼ cup chopped onion** (1.25 oz or 35 gm)

Mix together and bake uncovered at 350 degrees F (180 C) for 45 minutes.

4 servings, each: 124 cal, 7 g fat (0 sat.), 9 g carb (2 g fiber), 6 g protein

Broccoli Bacon Salad

- **1 cup mayonnaise** (240 ml)
- **2 Tb. white vinegar** (30 ml)
- **1 Tb. Splenda™ Granular** (15 ml)
- **1 tsp. salt** (5 ml)
- **½ tsp. black pepper** (2.5 ml)
- **1 head raw broccoli** (approximately 10 oz. or 280 gm)
- **8 oz. shredded cheddar cheese** (225 gm)
- **8 oz. cooked crumbled bacon** (225 gm)

Whisk together mayonnaise, vinegar, Splenda™, salt, and pepper. Chop broccoli into small pieces and add to dressing. Just before serving, stir in bacon and cheese.

8 servings, each: 439 cal, 40 g fat (7 sat.), 3 g carb (1 g fiber), 16 g protein

Cabbage Noodles

- **½ head Napa or green cabbage** (approx. 6 cups, 1200 ml, raw - I prefer the milder flavor of Napa, or "Chinese" cabbage, personally.)
- **1 Tb. heavy cream** (15 ml)
- **6 cups of water** (1.5 liters)

Bring water to a boil. Add sliced cabbage and cream. Boil just until cabbage is tender-crisp, perhaps eight to ten minutes. Drain and serve. (Adding the cream while boiling removes some of the sour taste from the cabbage and also reduces cooking odors. If cabbage odors remain, leave a dish of plain white vinegar out on the counter overnight.) Also good when simply stir fried with a little oil.

4 servings, each: 28 cal, 2 g fat (0 sat.), 2 g carb (1 g fiber), 0 g protein

Egg Noodles

- **6 large eggs**
- **¼ cup cream** (60 ml)
- **¼ tsp. salt** (1.5 ml)
- **½ tsp. pepper** (2.5 ml)

Whisk all ingredients together briskly, then add to warm, buttered pan one half cup at a time. Cook over low heat until set but not browned, then carefully flip and cook the opposite side. Repeat with all remaining batter, stacking the cooked "pancakes" until all are cooked. Slice into noodle shapes and add to soups or use as a base for sauces or main dishes.

2 servings, each: 265 cal, 19 g fat (6 sat.), 2 g carb, 19 g protein

Cheese Pots

Not a soufflé, and not a quiche, these tasty little sides have deep brown, chewy crusts and a decadent, creamy, middle.

- **½ cup diced Swiss cheese** (4 oz. or 115 gm)
- **½ cup Parmesan cheese** (120 ml)
- **3 egg yolks**
- **2/3 cup heavy cream** (160 ml)
- **½ tsp. black pepper** (2.5 ml)

Beat egg yolks with cream and pepper. Divide cheeses evenly between four individual, greased ramekins or custard dishes, and pour egg mixture over cheese. Bake at 350 F. (180 C) for 40 minutes, until tops are a deep golden brown.

4 servings, each: 331 cal, 29 g fat (17 sat.), 2 g carb, 15 g protein

Creamed Cucumbers

- **1/2 onion – sliced thinly in rings** (200 gm)
- **4 medium cucumbers, sliced** (800 gm - may peel or not, as desired)
- **2 cups mayonnaise** (480 ml)
- **½ cup white vinegar** (120 ml)
- **1 Tb. Splenda™ Granular** (15 ml)
- **1 Tb. fresh ground black pepper** (15 ml)

Slice cucumbers and layer in a bowl, sprinkling each layer with salt. Cover and let set in refrigerator several hours or overnight. Drain accumulated water from cucumbers. (Rinse before using if you have any sodium restrictions, but if not, use as is). This procedure will make your cucumbers more tender and remove any bitterness. Whisk together remaining ingredients and pour over cucumbers. Sauce will thicken after standing a few hours and will continue to thicken and improve in flavor for several days.

12 servings, each: 392 cal, 37.5 g fat (5 sat.), 3 g carb (1 g fiber) - These numbers are unrealistically high, since you rarely eat all the sauce - try some of the leftover over a salad..

Creamy Cole Slaw

- **½ a small zucchini, grated** (4 oz. 115 gm, or ¾ cup 180 ml)
- **2 Tb. finely grated sweet red pepper** (30 ml)
- **1 Tb. finely grated onion** (15 ml)
- **½ head** (10 oz. - 280 gm or about 5 cups – 1200 ml) **shredded cabbage, I like to use Napa for a milder flavor, but regular green cabbage is traditional**
- **1 tsp. salt** (5 ml)
- **1 tsp. black pepper** (5 ml)
- **1½ cups mayonnaise** (360 ml)
- **2 Tb. white vinegar** (30 ml)
- **2 Tb. Splenda™ Granular** (30 ml)
- **2 Tb. sour cream** (30 ml)

Toss vegetables together lightly. Whisk remaining ingredients together and combine with vegetables. (You may substitute 16 oz. pre-mixed coleslaw mix (cabbage and carrots) for all the listed vegetables.)

8 servings, each: 318 cal, 34 g fat (4 g sat.), 2 g carb

Faux-Tato Chips

- **1 average white turnip, peeled and sliced paper thin**
- **Hot oil for deep frying**
- **Seasoned salt**

Slice turnip paper thin using a mandolin or food processor. Fry in hot oil until browned and crispy. Remove to drain on paper towels and sprinkle with seasoned salt.

These are tart and lively, a departure from potato chips for sure, but very good nevertheless. *A half cup of sliced turnips has only 18 cal, 0.65 g fat, 4 carbs (1 gm fiber) and 0.6 g protein, so you can eat a lot of these without any guilt!*

Garlic Mashed Faux-tatoes

- **1 head fresh cauliflower,** (about 3 cups or 720 ml, 16 oz, 450 gm)
- **1 cup water** (240 ml)
- **2 Tb. cream** (30 ml)
- **6 Tb. unsalted butter** (75 ml)
- **1/3 cup sour cream** (80 ml)
- **2 tsp. salt** (10 ml)
- **1 tsp. black pepper** (5 ml)
- **2 Tb. dry parsley** (30 ml)
- **1 tsp. minced garlic** (5 ml)

Cut cauliflower into chunks and puree in a food processor until it is the approximate size and consistency of rice. Add the cream to the water and pour over cauliflower. Microwave for ten minutes, covered, stirring once halfway through.

Pour cauliflower mixture into a fine mesh sieve and press out all the liquid that you can. Return solid mixture to food processor and add butter, sour cream, parsley, garlic, salt, and pepper.

Puree again until very creamy, and serve immediately.

4 servings, each: 222 cal, 22 g fat (13 sat.), 6 g carb (3 g fiber), 3 g protein

May substitute cream cheese for sour cream.

For twice-baked faux-tatoes, add **1 cup** (240 ml) shredded cheese, divide among individual ramekins, garnish with crumbled bacon bits, and bake in 350 degree F (180 C) oven till heated through and crispy on top, about 30 minutes.

Also delicious when the cheese is placed only on the top instead of mixed in.

Green Beans Almandine

- **4 cups crisp-cooked green beans** (1 liter – and I really think fresh green beans are essential for this.)
- **1/3 cup of the bean cooking water** (80 ml)
- **1/3 cup red wine vinegar** (80 ml)
- **1/3 cup extra virgin olive oil** (80 ml)
- **1 tsp. salt** (5 ml)
- **½ tsp. black pepper** (2.5 ml)
- **½ cup slivered almonds** (120 ml)
- **½ tsp. minced garlic** (2.5 ml)
- **1 tsp. fresh minced oregano or ½ tsp. dried leaf oregano** (5 ml fresh or 2.5 ml dried)

Clean beans and slice into one inch lengths. Plunge into boiling water for 5-7 minutes; cook until tender-crisp. Drain, reserving 1/3 cup of the cooking water.

Rinse beans under cold water, to stop the cooking process. Drain well.

Whisk together remaining ingredients, and pour over beans and almonds. Cover and refrigerate for at least 4 hours. Be sure to stir well occasionally while it is chilling, and just before serving, to distribute dressing.

Tastes best at room temperature.

8 half-cup servings, each: 129 cal, 13 g fat (1 sat.), 3 g carb , 2 g protein

Marinated Summer Salad

- **2 sweet bell peppers**
- **2 small zucchinis**
- **1 cucumber**
- **1 bunch green onions**
- **12 cherry tomatoes**
- **¼ cup olive oil** (60 ml)
- **¼ cup red wine vinegar** (60 ml)
- **2 Tb. Splenda Granular™** (30 ml)
- **3 Tb. water** (45 ml)
- **½ tsp. minced garlic** (2.5 ml)
- **1 tsp. black pepper** (5 ml)
- **½ tsp. salt** (2.5 ml)

Slice all vegetables in bite size pieces. I like to julienne the peppers, thinly slice the green onions, halve and slice the cucumbers and zucchinis, and quarter the cherry tomatoes.

Whisk together remaining ingredients and pour over vegetables. Cover and refrigerate for 24 hours before serving.

Nutritional counts will vary depending on size of vegetables - *8 servings, approximately: 150 cal, 14 g fat (1 sat.), 6 g carb (2 g fiber), 0 g protein*

Did you know ...

You can dress up and add interest to steamed vegetables by simply sprinkling them with toasted sesame or sunflower seeds, and/or toasted, chopped nuts before serving.

Mock-A-Roni and Cheese

- **16 oz. firm tofu** (450 gm)
- **1 head of cauliflower, about 3 cups** (720 ml)
- **4 cups of grated extra sharp cheddar** (1 liter)
- **4 eggs**
- **½ cup heavy whipping cream** (120 ml)
- **1 tsp. salt** (5 ml)
- **1 Tb. freshly ground pepper** (15 ml)
- **1 tsp. garlic powder** (5 ml)
- **1 Tb. parsley** (15 ml)
- **½ cup crushed pork rinds** (120 ml)
- **¼ cup Parmesan cheese** (60 ml)

Grease one large or two small casserole dishes, and preheat oven to 350 degrees F (180 C). Press and drain any excess water from the tofu in a paper-towel lined colander. Chop drained tofu and scatter in the casserole dish. Top with cooked bite size pieces of cauliflower, and grated cheese.
Beat eggs and cream with seasonings and pour over contents of casserole dish. Sprinkle parmesan cheese and crushed pork rind crumbs over the top. Bake 45-60 minutes, until top is well browned. If necessary or desired, place under broiler briefly to crisp top.

12 servings, each: 358 cal, 28 g fat (15 sat.), 5 g carb (1 g fiber), 22 g protein

You can replace the pork rinds on top with bacon bits, if desired.

I never tell anyone there is tofu in this dish, and everyone always likes it as-is. Try it, even if you think you hate tofu!

Rainbow Salad

- **16 ounces 'Rainbow Salad' mix: julienned mix of broccoli hearts, cauliflower hearts, carrots, red cabbage** (450 gm)
- **1 cup shredded cheddar cheese** (240 ml)
- **2 cups mayonnaise** (480 ml)
- **¼ cup red wine vinegar** (60 ml)
- **4 Tb. minced fresh parsley , or 2 Tb. dry** (60 ml fresh or 30 ml dry)
- **2 Tb. Splenda™ Granular** (30 ml)
- **1 tsp. onion powder** (5 ml)
- **1 tsp. seasoned salt** (5 ml)
- **½ tsp. garlic powder** (2.5 ml)
- **1 tsp. black pepper** (5 ml)
- **2 Tb. heavy whipping cream** (30 ml)

Simply toss vegetables and cheese in a large bowl. Whisk remaining ingredients separately, and adjust seasonings to taste. Mix and enjoy.

8 servings, each: 434 cal, 45 g fat (6 sat.), 4 g carb (1 g fiber), 0 g protein

<u>Variations</u>: If you can't find the pre-mix, consider grating the individual ingredients for a rustic coleslaw, or using broccoli slaw instead.
You might also enjoy adding:
- **Sliced green onions**
- **Diced black olives**
- **Sliced mushrooms**
- **Chopped sweet or hot peppers**
- **Chopped hardboiled eggs**
- **Fresh Herbs: Almost any fresh herb would enliven and improve this salad! I particularly enjoy summer savory, cilantro, or dillweed.**

Roasted Stuffed Red Peppers

A colorful vegetable dish that even my children were surprised to find that they liked.

- **4 sweet red peppers, roasted**
- **7 oz. fresh cauliflower** (200 gm -1 very small head or ½ a large head)
- **½ cup Parmesan cheese** (120 ml)
- **8 oz. cream cheese, softened** (225 gm)
- **¾ cup shredded mozzarella cheese** (180 ml)
- **10 oz. frozen chopped spinach, thawed** (280 gm)
- **¼ cup** (2 oz.) **grated onion** (60 gm/ml)
- **1 tsp. black pepper** (5 ml)

Roast peppers on grill, under broiler or directly over gas range flames until skins are completely blackened and charred. Place in a heavy-duty plastic and close. Allow peppers to rest in the bag for about 20 minutes, then peel skins off, and remove tops and seeds. Allow peppers to cool while you mix stuffing.

Squeeze all the excess water out of the thawed spinach. Chop the cauliflower in large pieces and then pulse in food processor till reduced to a fine rice-like consistency. It should measure about 1½ cups after mincing. Place spinach in a large bowl with cauliflower and all other remaining ingredients and mix well. Spoon stuffing mixture lightly into peppers.

Stand peppers upright in a small greased loaf pan and bake at 375 degrees F (190 C) for about an hour, until filling is cooked through and peppers are beginning to blacken on edges.

4 servings, each: 391 cal, 29 g fat (18 sat.), 14 g carb (5 g fiber), 20 g protein

Scalloped Turnips

These may look like, but they do not taste like, potatoes. Enjoy them for their own unique flavor.

- **2 large turnips, cut in half and then sliced** (16 oz. or 450 gm)
- **4 cups water** (1 liter)
- **1 Tb. salt** (15 ml)
- **½ cup sour cream** (120 ml)
- **½ cup buttermilk** (120 ml)
- **½ cup unsalted butter** (120 ml)
- **1 tsp. salt** (5 ml)
- **1 tsp. black pepper** (5 ml)

Mix the salt and the water. Soak sliced turnips in salt water for one hour. Drain, rinse, and dry turnips between paper towels. Oil bottom and sides of a 1 quart covered casserole. Slice butter into thin pats. Mix sour cream, buttermilk, 1 tsp. salt, and pepper, then layer in casserole with turnips and butter pats.

Bake at 350 degrees F (180 C) for 30 minutes, covered. Uncover and bake an additional 30 minutes.

6 servings, each: 175 cal, 16 g fat (9 sat.), 6 g carb (1 g fiber), 2 g protein

---

Did you know ...

You can reduce cooking odors when boiling cauliflower, turnips, or cabbage, by adding a little vinegar or heavy cream to the cooking water.

Stuffing

- **2 cups All-Bran™ Extra Fiber or Fiber One™ cereal** (480 ml)
- **2½ oz. crushed pork rinds, about 2 cups** (70 gm or 480 ml)
- **1½ - 2 cups chicken stock** (360 - 480 ml)
- **1 Tb. dried parsley** (15 ml)
- **½ cup chopped green onions** (120 ml, 2 oz, 60 gm)
- **4 stalks celery, diced fine** (about 2 oz. or 60 gm)
- **1 tsp. garlic powder** (5 ml)
- **2 tsp. ground sage** (10 ml)
- **½ cup Parmesan cheese** (120 ml)
- **¼ cup unsalted butter** (60 ml)

Sauté onion and celery in butter until softened. Do not brown. Mix cereal and pork rind crumbs with dry spices in a large bowl. Add butter and vegetables and mix. Toss with chicken stock until it holds together but is not soggy. Bake in a greased casserole dish in a 350 degree F (180 C) oven till thoroughly warmed, about 40 minutes, or use it to stuff a bird or butterflied pork chops or fish.

8 servings, each: 340 cal, 19 g fat (9 sat.), 24 g carb (15 g fiber), 16 g protein

You can lower the "net" carb count to 4 by reducing the cereal to 1 cup and substituting additional pork rinds, but the pork flavor will be very strong, too strong for me. I prefer to just recommend that you reserve this dish for special occasions or maintenance.

You can substitute 6 slices of cubed TLC Hearty Dark Bread for all the pork rinds. **In that case,** *each serving: 392 cal, 21 g fat (8 sat.), 36 g carb (18 g fiber), 15 g protein*

Did you know ...

✓ Seeds and nuts, whether shelled or in the shell, keep best in the freezer. Unshelled nuts crack more easily when frozen. You can use also nuts and seeds directly out of the freezer without having to thaw them.

✓ When boiling eggs, you can add some vinegar to the water to prevent white from leaking out of a cracked egg.

✓ You can eliminate mildew, dust and odors, by wiping down walls with a vinegar-soaked cloth.

✓ You can clean windows with vinegar and water.

✓ You can pour boiling vinegar down drains to un-clog and clean them.

✓ You can clean fireplace bricks with undiluted vinegar.

✓ You can add vinegar to boiling ham to improve flavor and cut salty taste.

✓ You can remove berry stains from hands with vinegar.

✓ You can soften hardened paint brushes with vinegar: simmer in boiling vinegar then wash in hot soapy water.

✓ Clean lunch boxes and food containers with a vinegar-dampened cloth to keep them fresh-smelling and clean.

TLC Bake Mix

ULTRA LOW CARB (ULC) BAKE MIX

- **4 cups (270 gm) soy protein isolate (960 ml)**
- **2 cups (200 gm) soy flour (480 ml)**
- **1½ cups (170 gm) oat flour (360 ml)**
- **1½ cups (140 gm) almond flour (360 ml)**
- **½ cup (70 gm) vital wheat gluten (120 ml)**
- **4 tsp. baking soda (20 ml)**
- **5 Tb. baking powder (75 ml)***
- **2 tsp. salt (10 ml)**

Yield: 10 cups - 501 cal, 24 g fat (0 sat.), 26 g carb (9 g fiber), 50 g protein, per cup.

MODERATE CARB (MC) BAKE MIX

- **3 cups (200 gm) protein isolate (720 ml)**
- **2 cups (200 gm) soy flour (480 ml)**
- **2½ cups (230 gm) oat flour (600 ml)**
- **1 cup (150 gm) whole wheat flour (240 ml)**
- **½ cup (70 gm) vital wheat gluten (120 ml)**
- **½ cup (70 gm) all purpose flour (120 ml)**
- **4 tsp. baking soda (20 ml)**
- **5 Tb. baking powder (75 ml)***
- **2 tsp. salt (10 ml)**

Yield: 10 cups - 374 cal, 6 g fat (0 sat.), 40 g carb (8 g fiber), 39 g protein, per cup.

SOY FREE (SF) BAKE MIX

- **4 cups (265 gm) whey protein isolate (960 ml.)**
- **2½ cups (230 gm) oat flour (600 ml)**
- **2 cups (190 gm) almond flour (480 ml)**
- **1 cup (140 gm) vital wheat gluten (240 ml)**
- **4 tsp. baking soda (20 ml)**
- **5 Tb. baking powder (75 ml)***
- **2 tsp. salt (10 ml)**

Yield: 10 cups - 540 cal, 27 g fat (0 sat.), 32 g carb (8 g fiber), 47 g protein, per cup.

* HIGH ALTITUDE: − *over 5000 feet* − *reduce baking powder to 4 Tb. No other adjustments should be necessary, but you may get better results by raising the oven temperature 15- 25 degrees (reduce baking time as needed).*

I suggest you sift the ingredients together. Sift the protein isolate before you measure, for most accurate results. I have provided actual weights here and if you have a kitchen scale (highly recommended!) you can weigh the ingredients out directly into the sieve and not even bother with measuring cups. Do insure that the leaveners and flours are all mixed evenly together.

Expect a bit of a mess as the isolates are a bit "static-y" and tend to fly around a lot in their natural state. The advantage of mixing it with the heavier flours in bulk this way is that once you do this, you can make many different recipes with the finished mix before you have to do it again! You should be able to substitute this for the flour and leavening agents in many of your own recipes - experiment! Do not limit yourself to just the recipes that I have provided herein.

All Purpose Pie Crust

- **1½ cups almond flour or other nut meal** (360 ml)
- **4 Tb. Splenda™ Granular** (60 ml)
- **1 egg white**

Mix together almond flour, Splenda™, and egg white. If mixture is too dry to form a ball, add water, a few drops at a time, until it reaches the proper consistency. Press dough into pie plate and up sides with wet fingers, forming a rim. For baked fillings, proceed according to recipe. For unbaked fillings, prick all over with fork and bake at 350 degrees F (180 C) for about 10 minutes. Cool. For savory quiches, etc., omit sweetener.

8 servings, each: 259 cal, 22.5 g fat (0 sat.), 9 g carb (5 g fiber) 9 g protein

Almond Biscotti

- **½ cup unsalted butter** (4 oz, 110 gm)
- **1 cup Splenda™ Granular** (240 ml)
- **2 egg whites**
- **2 Tb. SF almond flavored syrup** (30 ml)
- **5 tsp. baking powder *** (25 ml)
- **3½ cups almond flour** (840 ml)

Cream softened butter with Splenda™, then add almond syrup slowly, then the egg whites. Sprinkle baking powder and almond flour over all, and mix well. Turn out in an oblong shape onto a long piece of plastic wrap. Wrap the plastic wrap around the dough and press it firmly into a log shape. Seal and chill for at least one hour. Preheat oven to 350 degrees F (180 C). Unroll dough log onto lightly greased cookie sheet and bake for 40 minutes. Cool for 30 minutes, then slice diagonally into 30 portions. Dough will be a bit crumbly, so be gentle with it. Place on ungreased cookie sheet. Bake at 250 degrees F (120 C) for an additional 45 minutes. Carefully transfer to wire rack and cool thoroughly. Handle with care. These are a bit more fragile than I would have liked, but the wonderful appearance and taste makes up for it. I freeze them immediately and think they're delicious directly out of the freezer.

* HIGH ALTITUDE: *Reduce baking powder to 4 tsp. in all variations.*

30 servings, each: 181 cal, 16 g fat (1 sat.), 6 g carb (3 g fiber) 6 g protein

DROP COOKIES: You can also bake the batter as drop cookies. Just drop dough on baking sheet by teaspoonfuls and bake at 350 degrees F (180 C) for 12-15 minutes.

SHORTBREAD: Pack a double batch of un-chilled batter into a bundt style pan and bake for 45-50 minutes. Cool for ten minutes; unmold.

Blueberry Muffins

- **2 cups vanilla protein powder** (240 ml)
- ***1 Tb. baking powder** (15 ml)
- **1 tsp. salt** (5 ml)
- **2 eggs**
- **¾ cup Splenda granular** (180 ml)
- **½ cup melted butter** (120 ml)
- **½ cup cream** (120 ml)
- **1 cup blueberries, fresh or frozen** (240 ml)

**Preheat oven to 375 degrees F.
Line 18 muffin tins with paper liners, or grease well. Combine protein powder, baking powder, and salt, and set aside. Whisk together eggs, Splenda, melted butter, and half and half cream. Make a well in the dry ingredients and pour in the wet mixture. Stir just until the dry ingredients are well incorporated. Fold in berries. Scoop out into muffin tins and bake for 12-14 minutes, until they test done in the centers. Serve warm with plenty of real butter.** *You may substitute bake mix for the protein powder, baking powder, and salt.*
*HIGH ALTITUDE: *Reduce baking powder to 2 tsp.*

18 servings, each: 98 cal, 7 g fat (3 g sat.), 2 g carb, 6 g protein - **Made with ULC OR SF Bake mix:** *127 cal, 9 g fat (3 g sat.), 5 g carb (1 g fiber) 6 g protein each.* **Made with MC,** *113 cal, 7 g fat (3 g sat.), 6 g carb (1 g fiber) 5 g protein each.*

Did you know ...

Use an oiled ice cream scoop – the kind with the metal "sweep" to push out the contents - to portion out biscuit and muffin and cookie batters and your whole batch will always come out the same size.

Brownies

- **¾ cup unsalted butter** (6 oz or 170 gm)
- **1½ oz. unsweetened baking chocolate** (40 gm)
- **1 cup Splenda™ Granular** (240 ml)
- **4 eggs**
- **1 Tb. unsweetened cocoa powder** (15 ml)
- **½ cup SF chocolate flavor syrup** (120 ml)
- **1½ cups** *TLC Bake Mix* (360 ml)
- **1 cup chopped nuts** (240 ml - I use walnuts).

Preheat oven to 350 degrees F (180 C). Grease well or line bottom of greased 13" x 9" pan with greased parchment paper, leaving some extra sticking out at each end. Place chocolate and butter in large microwavable bowl and heat on high until the butter melts. Remove from oven and stir until chocolate has melted and is smooth. Add Splenda™, eggs, cocoa powder, and chocolate syrup and beat well until thoroughly combined. Fold in bake mix and nuts. Bake about 22-24 minutes. Cool thoroughly on a rack, then lift from pan using parchment paper and cut into pieces.

24 servings, each: **Made with ULC mix :***135 cal, 11.5 g fat (4 g sat.), 3 g carb (1g fiber) 5 g protein*
SF or MC mix*: +1 g carb and -1 g protein, each*

These brownies would be even better if frosted with a mixture of ¼ cup (60 ml) **unsweetened peanut butter, ½ cup cream cheese** (120 ml) **and 2 Tb.** (30 ml) **SF syrup - I recommend DaVinci Gourmet™ French Vanilla flavor.** Or you could swirl this mixture through the batter before baking. Or get really crazy, and do both!

Brownies Too

- **1 cup soy flour** (240 ml)
- **1 cup chocolate protein powder** (240 ml)
- **1 Tb. baking powder** (15 ml)
- **1 tsp. salt** (5 ml)
- **1 cup Splenda™ Granular** (240 ml)
- **½ cup softened unsalted butter** (120 ml)
- **3 eggs**
- **2 oz. melted unsweetened chocolate** (60 gm)
- **½ cup whipping cream** (120 ml)
- **2 Tb. SF vanilla syrup** (30 ml)
- **1 cup chopped nuts** (240 ml)

Preheat oven to 350 degrees F (180 C). Sift soy flour, shake mix, baking powder and salt together until well-mixed. In one of the bowls, cream butter and Splenda™. Add eggs one at a time, beating well after each. Stir in melted chocolate, syrup, and cream. Add flour mixture and walnuts and stir just till combined. Spread in an well oiled or parchment paper lined 9" x 9" cake pan and bake for about 30 minutes.

24 servings, each: 133 cal, 11 g fat (4 sat.), 4 g carb (1 g fiber) 6 g protein

Created just to "use up" some shake mix that I didn't care for as shakes...

Did you know ...

When baking with butter, use the paper wrappers to grease the pans you will be baking with.

Buttermilk Biscuits

- **2 cups** *TLC Bake Mix* (480 ml)
- **½ cup cold butter** (120 ml, 4 oz., 110 gm)
- **2 eggs**
- **¾ cup buttermilk** (180 ml)

Preheat oven to 400 degrees F (200 C). Spray or line eight muffin tins. Cut cold butter into bake mix using pastry cutter or two knives. Make a well in the dry ingredients. Beat eggs slightly with buttermilk and add to bowl. Mix just until dry ingredients are well incorporated. Scoop out into muffin tins and bake 20-25 minutes, until golden brown.

8 servings, each: **ULC** *- 256 cal, 19 g fat (7 g sat.), 7 g carb (2 g fiber) 15 g protein* **MC** *- 224 cal, 14.5 g fat (7 g sat.), 11 g carb (2 g fiber) 12 g protein* **SF** *- 260 cal, 20 g fat (7 g sat.), 9 g carb (2 g fiber) 13 g protein*

Sausage Biscuits

Add 1 pound browned, drained sausage, 2 cups shredded cheddar, and 1 Tb. garlic powder.

Cheese Biscuits

Add ½ tsp. garlic powder (2.5 ml), **½ tsp. Italian Seasoning** (2.5 ml), **¼ cup grated Parmesan cheese** (60 ml), **and ¾ cup grated sharp cheddar cheese** (180 ml) **to dry ingredients.**

TOPPING:

- **3 Tb. melted unsalted butter** (45 ml)
- **½ tsp. garlic powder** (2.5 ml)
- **½ tsp. Italian seasoning** (2.5 ml)

Mix together and brush over tops of hot biscuits just before serving.

8 servings, each: **ULC** *- 285 cal, 22 g fat (10 g sat.), 7 g carb (2 g fiber) 16 g protein* **MC** *- 253 cal, 18 g fat (7 g sat.), 10 g carb (2 g fiber) 13 g protein* **SF** *- 289 cal, 23 g fat (9 g sat.), 8 g carb (2 g fiber) 14 g protein*

Chocolate Coconut Bars

BOTTOM LAYER:

- **1½ oz. unsweetened baking chocolate** (40 gm)
- **2 Tb. unsalted butter** (30 ml)
- **1 Tb. heavy cream** (15 ml)
- **½ cup SF chocolate flavor syrup** (120 ml)
- **½ cup unsweetened dried coconut** (120 ml)
- **1 cup chopped macadamia nuts** (120 ml)
- **¼ cup chocolate protein powder** (60 ml)
- **¼ cup Splenda™ Granular** (60 ml)

Place chocolate and butter in large microwavable bowl and heat for 45-60 seconds, until butter is melted. Remove from oven and stir until chocolate is completely melted and smooth. Add coconut, SF syrup, Splenda™, nuts, and protein powder, and stir until smooth. Using a rubber spatula, transfer to pan and smooth and even out as much as possible. Place in freezer while you make top layer.

TOP LAYER:

- **16 oz. softened cream cheese** (450 gm)
- **¼ cup SF coconut flavor syrup** (60 ml)
- **1 cup unsweetened dried coconut** (240 ml)
- **1 cup chocolate protein powder** (240 ml)
- **½ cup Splenda™ Granular** (120 ml)

Beat cream cheese until smooth. Add remaining ingredients and mix well. Smooth gently over chilled first layer and refrigerate until firm enough to cut into 16 pieces.

16 servings, each: 246 cal, 22 g fat (10 g sat.), 4 g carb (1 g fiber) 10 g protein

Chocolate Crunch Bars

- **¼ cup unsalted butter** (60 ml)
- **2 Tb. cocoa powder** (30 ml, or 1½ oz. {40 gm} unsweetened baking chocolate, melted)
- **2 Tb. heavy cream** (30 ml)
- **2 Tb. peanut butter** (30 ml)
- **¾ cup Splenda Granular™** (180 ml)
- **2 Tb. SF vanilla flavor syrup** (30 ml)
- **1 cup puffed rice** (240 ml, and if you can find the smaller sized puffed millet, even better!)

Melt butter, then stir in remaining ingredients in the order listed. Press into bottom of buttered 9"x9" pan and freeze.

16 servings, each: 54 cal, 5 g fat (2 g sat.), 2 g carb

Creamy Chocolate Fudge

Add 4 oz. (115 gm) **softened cream cheese. Substitute chopped nuts for the puffed rice. Chill in refrigerator instead of freezer.**

24 servings, each: 84 cal, 8 g fat (2 g sat.), 2 g carb, 1 g protein

How about adding unsweetened coconut?
Slivered almonds or other nuts?
Chopped low carb white chocolate chunks?
Chopped, dried sour cherries or cranberries?
OR ALL OF THE ABOVE?

Chocolate Drop Cookies

- **½ cup unsalted butter** (120 ml)
- **1 cup Splenda™ Granular** (240 ml)
- **2 eggs**
- **2 oz. unsweetened baking chocolate** (60 gm)
- **½ tsp. vanilla extract** (2.5 ml)
- **2 Tb. heavy cream** (30 ml)
- **1 cup** TLC Bake Mix (240 ml)
- **1 cup chopped walnuts** (240 ml)

Preheat oven to 350 degrees F (180 degrees C). Cream butter and Splenda™ together. Add eggs, melted chocolate, heavy cream, and vanilla extract and blend well. Stir in bake mix and nuts just until evenly mixed. Drop by teaspoonfuls onto greased baking sheet and bake for 10 minutes. Do not over-bake. Allow to cool on baking sheet for two minutes before removing to a rack to cool. These cookies reminded us of brownies and are best when very fresh.

36 servings, each: 75 cal, 7 g fat (1 g sat.), 2 g carb, 2 g protein

Chocolate Hazelnut Dreams

- **1 cup hazelnut butter** (240 ml)
- **2 Tb. oil** (30 ml—I used walnut)
- **3 Tb. cocoa powder** (45 ml)
- **1 cup granular Splenda** (240 ml)
- **4 Tb. SF hazelnut flavored syrup** (60 ml)
- **1 cup** TLC Bake Mix (240 ml)

Combine ingredients and roll into 20 small balls. Flatten slightly and bake at 375 F (180 C) **on ungreased cookie sheets for about 8 minutes.**

20 servings, each: **ULC OR SF:** *120 cal, 10 g fat (0 g sat.), 4 g carb (1 g fiber) 4 g protein* **MC:** *114 cal, 9 g fat (0 g sat.), 5 g carb (1 g fiber) 4 g protein*

Chocolate Pie

CRUST

- **1½ cups almond flour** (360 ml)
- **2 Tb. Splenda™ Granular** (30 ml)
- **2 Tb. unsweetened cocoa powder** (30 ml)
- **1 egg white**

Preheat oven to 350 degrees F (180 C). Mix together almond flour, cocoa powder, and egg white. If mixture is too dry to form a ball, add water, a few drops at a time, until it reaches the proper consistency. Press dough into pie plate and up sides with wet fingers, forming a rim. Prick all over with fork and bake for 10-12 minutes. Cool.

PIE FILLING

- **3 eggs + 1 egg yolk**
- **3 Tb. ThickenThin NotSugar™** (45 ml)
- **1½ cups Splenda™ Granular** (360 ml)
- **½ tsp. salt** (2.5 ml)
- **3 oz. melted unsweetened chocolate** (85 gm)
- **1 cup heavy whipping cream** (240 ml)
- **2 cups water** (480 ml)
- **1 tsp. vanilla extract** (5 ml)

Whisk together eggs and NotSugar™ until smooth, then add remaining ingredients, except for vanilla extract, adding liquids slowly. Heat, stirring constantly, over medium heat, until mixture comes to a rolling boil. Boil for one minute, remove from heat, add vanilla, then pour into baked pie crust. Lay plastic wrap directly on surface of filling and refrigerate until firm.

12 servings, each: 319 cal, 28 g fat (5 g sat.), 13 g carb (8 g fiber), 9 g protein

PUDDING VARIATION: Omit the crust, and divide into eight individual portions of pudding.

8 servings, each: 219 cal, 20 g fat (7 g sat.), 10 g carb (3 g fiber), 4 g protein

Chocolate Snack Cake

- **6 oz. unsweetened baking chocolate** (170 gm)
- **1 cup unsalted butter** (240 ml)
- **3 eggs**
- **1 cup heavy cream** (240 ml)
- **1 cup water** (240 ml)
- **2 cups Splenda™ Granular** (480 ml)
- **1 cup soy flour** (240 ml - can use other flours)
- **2 Tb. vital wheat gluten** (30 ml)
- **1 tsp. baking soda** (5 ml)
- **1 cup All-Bran™ Extra Fiber cereal** (240 ml)
- **1 cup chopped walnuts** (240 ml)

Preheat oven to 350 degrees F (180 C). Place butter and chocolate in a microwave-proof bowl and heat just till the butter is melted. Remove from oven and stir until chocolate is completely melted and smooth. Add eggs and beat well. Stir in cream and water. Set aside. In another bowl, sift together Splenda™, soy flour, wheat gluten and baking soda. Add cereal and wet ingredients, and mix just till combined. Spread in greased 13"x 9" pan. Sprinkle walnuts over the top and bake until a toothpick inserted in the center of the cake comes out clean and the top springs back when touched lightly – about 30 minutes.

24 servings, each: 212 cal, 19 g fat (7 g sat.), 8 g carb (3 g fiber), 4 g protein

Cinnamon Coffee Cake

CAKE:
- **1 cup softened unsalted butter** (240 ml)
- **½ cup non-hydrogenated shortening** (120 ml - may also use coconut oil or additional butter)
- **1½ cups Splenda™ Granular** (360 ml)
- **1 Tb. blackstrap molasses** (15 ml)
- **1 egg + 2 egg whites**
- **2 cups** TLC Bake Mix (480 ml)
- **1 cup sour cream** (240 ml)

TOPPING:
- **½ cup Splenda™ Granular** (120 ml)
- **1 Tb. unsalted melted butter** (15 ml)
- **1 tsp. ground cinnamon** (5 ml)
- **1 cup chopped walnuts** (120 ml)

Preheat oven to 350 degrees F (180 C). Grease a 9" x 13" pan and use 2 Tb. of the bake mix to flour the bottom and sides of the pan. Mix topping ingredients and set aside. Cream butter, shortening, and Splenda™ with molasses. Add eggs and mix well. Add dry ingredients to wet ingredients alternately with sour cream. (Add one third of the dry, half of the sour cream, another one third of dry, remaining sour cream, then remaining dry, mixing after each addition). Spread in pan and sprinkle walnut topping over the top. Bake until a toothpick inserted in the center of the cake comes out clean and the top springs back when touched lightly – about 40-50 minutes.

18 servings, each: 208 cal, 18 g fat (8 g sat.), 5 g carb (1 g fiber), 7 g protein

RHUBARB VARIATION: Fold 1.5 cups diced rhubarb into batter just being spreading in pan. *Adds 1 g carb and 4 calories per serving.*

Classic Cheesecakes

CRUST
- **3 cups All-Bran™ Extra Fiber cereal** (720 ml)
- **1/3 cup Splenda™ Granular** (80 ml)
- **2 Tb. unsweetened cocoa powder** (30 ml)
- **½ cup melted unsalted butter** (120 ml)

Preheat oven to 450 degrees F (200 C). Mix cereal crumbs, Splenda™, and cocoa powder in spring-form pan. Pour melted butter over all, and press evenly into bottom and up sides of pan with your fingers. Place pan in freezer to chill while preparing filling.

FILLING
- **2 lbs. cream cheese** (900 gm)
- **2 eggs**
- **1½ cups Splenda™ Granular** (360 ml)
- **1 tsp. pure vanilla extract** (5 ml)
- **½ tsp. almond extract** (2.5 ml)
- **1 cup sour cream** (240 ml)

Beat room temperature cream cheese until very smooth, scraping down beaters and sides of bowl at least once. Slowly add the Splenda, beating well. Add eggs, one at a time, scraping sides and beating well after each addition. Add the sour cream and vanilla and almond extracts and mix well. Pour into chilled crust and bake at 450 degrees F for 10 minutes. Reduce oven temperature to 250 degrees F (120 C) and bake another 50 minutes. Cool on a rack until it reaches room temperature, then place in refrigerator to thoroughly chill. Once chilled, you can easily remove the pan sides.

16 servings, each: 343 cal, 29 g fat (17 g sat.), 13 g carb (5 g fiber), 7 g protein

TIPS FOR TROUBLE FREE CHEESECAKES

✓ This recipe works best in a 10" spring-form pan, easily found and inexpensive. But if you are un-willing to invest in a new pan, simply bake this in a deep-dish pie pan or a 9x9 pan. You may end up with too much filling if you use a pie pan. Just bake it alongside in a buttered oven-proof bowl. It will be the chef's own taste treat!

✓ Allow all ingredients to come to room tempera-ture before beginning.

✓ Scrape the bowl often and insure that you have no lumps in your batter at any step in this proc-ess, and you will be rewarded with a cheese-cake whose top is smooth and without cracks.

✓ You can always skip the crust completely, to re-duce carbs. Just butter the pan very well.

✓ Don't overmix the batter, too much air in the batter can cause surface cracks in the finished cheesecake.

VARIATIONS

✓ Make this into a chocolate cheesecake by omit-ting the almond extract and adding 4 ounces melted unsweetened baking chocolate plus ad-ditional sweetener to taste (I use 1/2 cup).

✓ Reduce cereal in crust to 1½ cups (360 ml) and add 1½ cups (360 ml) finely chopped nuts, or use all nuts. Macadamias are especially good in this crust.

✓ Cheesecakes can be topped with pureed berries and whipped cream, TLC Jelly or Jam, or my fa-vorite: 2 oz. (60 gm) melted unsweetened bak-ing chocolate mixed with 1/2 cup Splenda™ Granular (120 ml), 1 tsp. instant coffee granules (5 ml), and 2 Tb. (30 ml) heavy cream. Do not top until well chilled.

Coconut Cream Pie

CRUST
- **1 cup almond flour** (240 ml)
- **1 cup unsweetened coconut** (240 ml)
- **1 egg white**

Preheat oven to 350 degrees F (180 C). Mix together almond flour, coconut, and egg white. If mixture is too dry to form a ball, add water a few drops at a time until it reaches the proper consistency. Press into pie plate and up sides with wet fingers, forming a rim.

PIE FILLING
- **3 eggs**
- **3 Tb. ThickenThin NotSugar™** (45 ml)
- **1 cup pure coconut milk** (240 ml)
- **1 cup unsweetened coconut** (240 ml)
- **½ cup Splenda™ Granular** (120 ml)
- **¼ cup SF coconut syrup** (60 ml)
- **¼ cup buttermilk** (60 ml)
- **2 Tb. sour cream** (30 ml)

Whisk together eggs and NotSugar™ until smooth, then add remaining ingredients. Pour into pie crust and bake for about 45 minutes. Cool on wire rack.

8 servings, each: 314 cal, 27 g fat (8 g sat.), 11 g carb (6 g fiber), 10 g protein

---

Did you know ...

fabric softener sheets will prevent thread from tangling? Run a threaded needle through a sheet of fabric softener sheet to eliminate the static cling on the thread before sewing.

Cranberry Orange Bread

- **½ cup Splenda™ Granular** (120 ml)
- **1 egg**
- **1/3 cup buttermilk** (80 ml)
- **½ cup SF vanilla syrup** (120 ml)
- **¼ cup orange juice** (60 ml)
- **1 Tb. orange zest** (15 ml)
- **2½ cups** *TLC Bake Mix* (600 ml)
- **½ cup cranberries, minced** (120 ml)

Preheat oven to 350 degrees F (180 C). Combine all ingredients in mixing bowl in order listed and blend just till moistened. Bake about 40 minutes in well greased loaf pan, until a toothpick inserted in the center comes out clean.

16 servings, each: **ULC:** *94 cal, 4 g fat (0 g sat.), 6 g carb (1 g fiber), 8 g protein* **MC:** *74 cal, 1 g fat (0 g sat.), 8 g carb (1 g fiber), 6 g protein* **SF:** *96 cal, 5 g fat (0 g sat.), 7 g carb (1 g fiber), 7 g protein*

Lemon Poppy Seed Bread

Substitute **¼ cup** (60 ml) **poppy seeds for the cranberries and lemon juice/zest for the orange juice/zest.**

16 servings, each: **ULC:** *112 cal, 6 g fat (0 g sat.), 6 g carb (2 g fiber), 9 g protein* **MC:** *92 cal, 3 g fat (0 g sat.), 9 g carb (2 g fiber), 7 g protein* **SF:** *114 cal, 6 g fat (0 g sat.), 7 g carb (2 g fiber), 7 g protein*

Pumpkin Bread

Substitute **canned pumpkin for the cranberries. Omit lemon juice/zest. Add ¼ tsp. ground cloves** (1.25 ml)**, 1 tsp. ground cinnamon** (5 ml)**, ¼ tsp. ground ginger** (1.25 ml)**, and ¼ tsp.** (1.25 ml) **allspice.**

16 servings, each: **ULC:** *91 cal, 4 g fat (0 g sat.), 5 g carb (1 g fiber), 8 g protein* **MC:** *71 cal, 1 g fat (0 g sat.), 8 g carb (1 g fiber), 6 g protein* **SF:** *94 cal, 5 g fat (0 g sat.), 6 g carb (1 g fiber), 7 g protein*

Deep Dark Chocolate Fudge Cake

- **2 cups almond flour** (480 ml)
- **1¾ cups Splenda™ Granular** (420 ml)
- **½ cup Dutch style cocoa powder** (120 ml)
- **2 tsp. baking soda** (10 ml)
- **2 tsp. baking powder*** (10 ml)
- **1 tsp. salt** (5 ml)
- **2 eggs**
- **¾ cups cream** (180 ml)
- **½ cup SF syrup** (120 ml -any complimentary flavor)
- **½ cup oil** (120 ml)
- **2 tsp. vanilla extract** (10 ml)

Whisk ingredients together in order listed and place in very well greased pans.

Bake at 350 for about 14 minutes for 18 cupcakes, 30 minutes for a 9x 13, 20 minutes for two round layers, and 35 minutes for one bundt pan.

* High Altitude: Reduce baking soda to 1½ tsp. (7.5 ml).
16 servings, each: 241 cal, 22 g fat (1 g sat.), 8 g carb (3 g fiber), 7 g protein

TUNNEL OF FUDGE CAKE VARIATION: Cream together 8 oz. cream cheese (225 gm), 1 cup nut butter (240 ml), 1 cup Splenda Granular (240 ml), and 3 Tb. (45 ml) SF syrup (in a complimentary flavor of your choice). Add 2/3 of the batter to the pan, then carefully spoon the filling in a ring around the center of the pan on top of the batter. Top with the remaining batter, and bake as directed. *This adds 1-2 carbs per serving depending on nut butter used.*

GLAZE SUGGESTION: The topping layer (without the nuts) from the Peanut Nirvana recipe makes a wonderful shiny glaze for this cake. *Adds 1 additional carb per serving.*

Flax Muffins

- **1 cup boiling water** (240 ml)
- **4 Tb. ground flax seeds** (60 ml)
- **2½ cups** *TLC Bake Mix* (360 ml)
- **½ cup Splenda™ Granular** (120 ml)
- **4 Tb. buttermilk** (60 ml)
- **½ cup oil** (120 ml)
- **4 eggs**
- **1/3 cup sour cream** (80 ml)
- **½ cup SF syrup** (120 ml, any flavor desired)

Pour boiling water over flax seed and set aside for five minutes to soften.

In a large bowl, beat together buttermilk, eggs, oil, sour cream, syrup, softened flax seeds, and Splenda.

Add bake mix and stir just till moistened.

Divide among 24 well greased or paper-lined muffin tins and bake at 375 F (180 C) **for about 20 minutes.**

TOPPING:
- **1 oz. unsweetened baking chocolate** (28 gm)
- **2 Tb. unsalted butter** (30 ml)
- **1/3 cup Splenda granular** (80 ml)
- **3 Tb. SF syrup, any flavor desired** (45 ml)

Melt unsweetened baking chocolate with butter. Stir in SF syrup and Splenda granular. Drizzle or spoon over tops of cooled muffins.

24 servings, each: **ULC:** *133 cal, 10 g fat (1 g sat.), 3 g carb (0 g fiber), 8 g protein* **MC:** *125 cal, 9 g fat (1 g sat.), 4 g carb (1 g fiber), 7 g protein* **SF:** *134 cal, 10 g fat (1 g sat.), 3 g carb (1 g fiber), 8 g protein*

Fruity Bread Pudding

- **½ cup Splenda™ Granular** (120 ml)
- **1 cup softened unsalted butter** (240 ml)
- **¼ cup SF vanilla syrup** (60 ml)
- **4 eggs**
- **1 tsp. ground cinnamon** (5 ml)
- **¼ tsp. ground cloves** (1.25 ml)
- **½ cup heavy cream** (120 ml)
- **1½ cups** *TLC Bake Mix* (360 ml)
- **2½ to 3 cups chopped fruits and berries –** (600-750 gm, you may use fresh or frozen. I analyzed an equal combination of rhubarb and blueberry. All strawberry is delicious too.)

Generously grease and flour (flour using bake mix, of course) an 8" tube pan. Put a pan on the stove with a rack and two inches of water in it and turn up the heat to high. Make sure your rack is level (even an overturned bowl will work) and that the pan is large enough to hold your tube pan. Cream softened butter and Splenda™ together. Slowly add vanilla syrup, scraping down beaters and sides of bowl often. Butter may seize up into small globs when you add the syrup. This is to be expected. Add eggs, one at a time, beating well and scraping sides after each addition. Add bake mix and cream alternately. Mixture should resemble oatmeal cookie dough. Fold in desired mixture of fruit, and spoon into prepared pan. Cover pan tightly with a piece of oiled aluminum foil and place on rack. Lower heat and steam for 60-90 minutes, until a toothpick inserted in the center comes out clean. Cool in pan on wire rack for ten minutes; then invert onto rack.

12 servings, each: **ULC:** *279 cal, 25 g fat (13 g sat.), 6 g carb (1 g fiber), 9 g protein* **MC:** *263 cal, 23 g fat (13 g sat.), 7 g carb (1 g fiber), 7 g protein* **SF:** *281 cal, 25 g fat (13 g sat.), 6 g carb (1 g fiber), 8 g protein*

Serve warm with *TLC Berri-Licious Syrup* and a drizzle of heavy cream over the top for true decadence. **115**

Fudgesicles

- **8 oz. cream cheese** (225 gm)
- **½ cup heavy cream** (120 ml)
- **½ cup half and half cream** (120 ml)
- **1 cup Splenda™ Granular** (240 ml)
- **½ oz. unsweetened baking chocolate** (15 gm)

Whip heavy cream until stiff and set aside. Beat cream cheese with half and half cream and Splenda™ until very smooth, scraping sides of bowl and beaters as needed. Fold in melted baking chocolate and whipped cream. Divide among popsicle molds and freeze. If you don't have or can't find the molds, you can make do with tiny juice glasses and spoons or sticks!

12 servings, each: 127 cal, 12 g fat (7 g sat.), 3 g carb, 2 g protein

Root Beer or Orange Creamsicles

Actually, the potential flavor combinations are almost endless. Just omit the chocolate and substitute 2 tsp. (10 ml) of your favorite flavoring extract. Or you could use a half-cup (120 ml) of sugar free flavored syrup and reduce the Splenda™ by a half cup, reducing carbs even further. If you're one of those people who likes peanut butter in everything, add ¼ cup (60 ml) of peanut butter to the cream cheese.

Heavenly Mousse

- **1 cup heavy whipping cream** (240 ml)
- **8 oz. cream cheese** (225 gm)
- **2 Tb. unsweetened peanut butter** (30 ml)
- **1 Tb. unsweetened cocoa powder** (15 ml)
- **1 cup Splenda™ Granular** (240 ml)

Allow cream cheese to come to room temperature before beginning. This is easiest to make in a stand mixer. Beat heavy whipping cream until peaks form, and set aside. Be careful - If you over do this step, you'll make butter! Beat cream cheese by itself for several minutes until very smooth, scraping down sides of bowl and beaters as needed. Add Splenda™, peanut butter and cocoa powder. Mix very well, scraping down beaters and sides again. Incorporate one scoop of the whipped cream into the cream cheese mixture first, to lighten it. Then, by hand, using a wide rubber spatula, fold in remaining whipped cream. Do not over mix, it is okay if you can still see veins of white streaking the mix. Cover with plastic wrap and refrigerate. Try to eat just ONE, okay. (That's one serving, not one batch.)

6 servings, each: 303 cal, 29 g fat (17 g sat.), 7 g carb , 4 g protein

Carbs can be reduced by using only half as much cream, or substituting sugar free syrup for some of the Splenda™. By omitting the chocolate and peanut butter and substituting extracts or sugar free syrup, the flavor combinations are practically endless! Experiment and find your favorite.

I have had the best results using 3-4 Tb. (45 - 60 ml) **of SF DaVinci Gourmet™ syrups. I like to make raspberry mousse and add ripe berries, or peach, with fresh diced peaches added. You could also add nuts, unsweetened coconut, etc.**

Hearty Dark Bread

In a large measuring cup, measure out:

- **1 cup hot water** (240 ml)
- **½ cup cream** (120 ml)
- **4 Tb. oil** (60 ml)
- **1 Tb. molasses** (15 ml)
- **1 egg**

Beat this mixture lightly; pour into bread machine.
Mix together:

- **1 cup vital wheat gluten** (240 ml - 140 g)
- **½ cup wheat bran** (120 ml - 30 g)
- **¼ cup oat bran** (60 ml - 25 g)
- **¼ cup whole grain wheat flour** (60 ml, 30 g)
- **¼ cup rye flour** (60 ml - 30 g)
- **¼ cup barley flour** (60 ml - 25 g)
- **¼ cup unsalted pumpkin seeds, ground** (60 ml)
- **¼ cup unsalted sunflower kernels, ground** (60 ml)
- **¼ cup flax seeds, ground** (60 ml)

Add pre-mixed dry ingredients to machine on top of wet ingredients, Do not mix, just pour it right on top. Make a small well in the top of the flours and add to well:

- **1.5 tsp. dry yeast*** (7.5 ml)

Try baking on rapid whole wheat setting with medium or dark crust baking option first, if available. Measure your ingredients carefully. I suggest using only organic, stone ground, whole flours. You may use all wheat bran, or all oat bran, if desired. You may use any combinations of seeds in order to make up the total 3/4 cup required. Measure seeds first, then grind.

May also be made in a mixer or by hand. May require small adjustments depending on your climate and ingredients, but getting it right will be worth your efforts!

*HIGH ALTITUDE: Reduce yeast by 1/4 tsp.

24 servings, each: 102 cal, 6 g fat (1 g sat.), 7 g carb (1 g fiber) , 6 g protein

Ice Cream

The simplest version - just stir together liquid ingredients, then freeze according to ice cream maker's directions.

VANILLA
- **1 cups heavy cream** * (240 ml)
- **2-1/2 cups half and half cream** (600 ml)
- **½ cup SF vanilla or French vanilla syrup** (120 ml)

4 servings, each: 402 cal, 40 g fat (24 g sat.), 6 g carb , 5 g protein

CHOCOLATE
- **1½ cups heavy cream** *(360 ml)
- **1 cup half and half cream** (240 ml)
- **1 cup SF chocolate syrup** (240 ml)
- **2 Tb. unsweetened cocoa powder** (30 ml)

4 servings, each: 392 cal, 40 g fat (25 g sat.), 5 g carb , 4 g protein

STRAWBERRY, ETC.
- **1½ cups heavy cream** * (360 ml)
- **1 cup half and half cream** (240 ml)
- **1 cup SF strawberry syrup** (240 ml)
- **2 tsp. vanilla extract** (10 ml)
- **3 Tb. water** (45 ml)
- **½ cup diced fresh strawberries** (120 ml - try peaches with peach syrup, etc.)

4 servings, each: 403 cal, 40 g fat (24 g sat.), 7 g carb ,3g protein

You get the idea – and there are so many different flavors of sugar free syrups available, you could invent a new flavor every time!

*You can replace some or all of the heavy cream with unsweetened yogurt, if you find the basic recipe too rich. (Adjust carbs as needed. I count yogurt carbs as less than the label, personally, meaning no real change for me. See _GO-Diet_ for details on the yogurt exception.)

Layered Fudge

BOTTOM LAYER:

- **3 oz. unsweetened baking chocolate, melted** (85 gm)
- **4 Tb. heavy whipping cream** (60 ml)
- **2 Tb. SF vanilla flavor syrup** (30 ml)
- **¼ cup peanut butter** (60 ml)
- **1 cup Splenda™ Granular** (240 ml)
- **1 cup chopped or sliced nuts** (240 ml)

Butter bottom and sides of 11x7 or 9x9 pan. Melt baking chocolate in microwave by heating on high for 30 seconds, then stirring, heating and stirring each 30 seconds thereafter until chocolate is smooth. Add remaining ingredients to chocolate, blend thoroughly, and transfer to buttered pan. Smooth and even out as much as possible using a rubber spatula. Chill in freezer while you make top layer.

TOP LAYER:

- **16 oz. softened cream cheese** (450 gm)
- **½ cup peanut butter** (120 ml)
- **¾ cup Splenda™ Granular** (180 ml)
- **2 Tb. SF vanilla flavor syrup** (30 ml)

Beat cream cheese until smooth. Add remaining ingredients and mix well. Smooth gently over chilled first layer and refrigerate until firm enough to cut into pieces.

32 servings, each: 133 cal, 12 g fat (4 g sat.), 4 g carb (1 g fiber), 3 g protein

Lemon Meringue Pie

CRUST: I use and included for analysis the All Purpose crust on page 97.

PIE FILLING
- **6 Tb. ThickenThin NotSugar™** (75 ml)
- **1½ cups Splenda™ Granular** (360 ml)
- **½ tsp. salt** (2.5 ml)
- **1½ cups water** (360 ml)
- **4 egg yolks**
- **2 Tb. unsalted butter** (30 ml)
- **1 Tb. lemon zest** (15 ml)
- **2 Tb. fresh lemon juice** (30 ml)

Whisk together Splenda™, NotSugar™, salt, and water over medium heat until it boils. Lower heat and cook for two minutes more. Remove from heat. Beat egg yolks slightly and slowly add about ¼ cup (60 ml) of the hot mixture to them, stirring rapidly all the while. Add another ¼ cup of the hot mixture to further warm the egg yolks, and then add it all to saucepan. Return to heat and boil two more minutes. Remove from heat and add butter, lemon juice, and lemon zest. Pour into cooled crust.

MERINGUE
- **3 egg whites**
- **½ cup Splenda™ Granular** (120 ml)
- **½ tsp. cream of tartar** (2.5 ml)
- **1½ tsp. vanilla extract** (7.5 ml)

Beat egg whites with remaining ingredients until stiff, and spread over hot lemon filling, making sure to completely cover filling and touching crust on all sides to seal and prevent shrinking while baking. Bake at 350 F (180 C) for about 15 minutes, until meringue is golden brown.

8 servings, each: 345 cal, 28 g fat (2 g sat.), 15 g carb (8 g fiber), 12 g protein

Maple Nut Cake

- **6 eggs**
- **½ tsp. cream of tartar** (2.5 ml)
- **1 cup Splenda™ Granular** (240 ml)
- **1 Tb. blackstrap molasses** (15 ml)
- **1½ tsp. maple extract** (7.5 ml)
- **½ cup SF maple flavor syrup** (120 ml)
- **2 cups pecan meal** (480 ml)

Preheat oven to 350 degrees F (180 C). **Oil two round cake pans. Line with parchment or waxed paper and oil top of paper also. Separate eggs carefully. Beat egg whites with cream of tartar until stiff; set aside. Beat egg yolks until thick and lemon colored. Add Splenda™, molasses, and maple extract, and mix well. Add maple syrup and pecan meal, scraping down sides of bowl and mixing thoroughly. Gently fold in egg whites and divide between the two pans. Bake 20 – 25 minutes, until a toothpick inserted in the center of the pan comes out clean. Cool on wire rack in pan for 5 minutes. Run a knife around the edge of the pan to loosen sides of cake. Invert over wire racks and remove pans. Allow to cool completely before frosting.**

Frosting

- **16 oz. softened cream cheese** (450 gm)
- **¼ cup heavy whipping cream** (60 ml)
- **1 cup Splenda™ Granular** (240 ml)
- **2 tsp. maple extract** (10 ml)
- **2 Tb. SF maple flavor syrup** (30 ml)
- **1 cup chopped nuts** (240 ml - I prefer walnuts)

Whip cream until stiff and set aside. Cream softened cream cheese with Splenda™. Gradually beat in maple syrup and maple flavoring. Fold in whipped cream and nuts, if using them. Frosts two layers, one 9x13, or 18 cupcakes. Keep refrigerated.

12 servings, each: 434 cal, 41 g fat (9 g sat.), 11 g carb (3 g fiber) , 10 g protein

122

Nirvana Bars

My favorite low carb creation of all time!

BOTTOM LAYER:

- **4 Tb. unsalted butter** (60 ml)
- **½ cup unsweetened peanut butter** (120 ml)
- **1 cup Splenda™ Granular** (240 ml - may omit)
- **1 cup vanilla protein powder** (240 ml)
- **2 cups sliced Brazil nuts, sliced almonds, or chopped walnuts** (480 ml)
- **2 – 4 Tb. SF French vanilla syrup** (30 – 60 ml)

Place melted butter in large bowl. Add peanut butter, Splenda™, protein powder, and nuts, and mix thoroughly. Mixture should be very dry. Drizzle the syrup over this mixture and stir. It should begin sticking together at this point. Depending on shake mix used, you may need to add more syrup to achieve the proper consistency. As soon as you can make it stick together, it is ready. Press it evenly into the bottom of a 13x9" pan. Put the pan in the freezer while you make the next layer.

MIDDLE LAYER:

- **16 oz. softened cream cheese** (450 gm)
- **½ cup peanut butter** (120 ml)
- **2 Tb. SF French vanilla syrup** (30 ml)
- **¾ cup vanilla protein powder** (180 ml)

Beat cream cheese until smooth. Add remaining ingredients and mix well. Spread evenly over chilled bottom layer.

(recipe continued next page)

TOP LAYER:
- **1 cup melted unsalted butter** (240 ml)
- **2 Tb. cocoa powder** (30 ml)
- **½ cup Splenda™ Granular** (120 ml)
- **2 Tb. SF French vanilla syrup** (30 ml)
- **1 cup sliced/chopped nuts** (240 ml- optional)

Mix, then spread out evenly, using back of spoon, until entire surface is evenly covered. Freeze pan again until they are firm enough to cut easily, about an hour.
I like to wrap these individually and keep them in the freezer. May be eaten frozen or refrigerated.

I like sliced Brazil nuts best but I have made it with chopped walnuts, pecans, sliced almonds, etc. and I always get great results. I often skip the nuts in the top layer and the sweetener in the crust layer.
48 servings, each: 172 cal, 16 g fat (6 g sat.), 3 g carb, 5 g protein (including nuts and all the sweetener.)

Chocolate Variation

BOTTOM LAYER: Omit peanut butter. Use chocolate shake powder and syrups instead of vanilla. Add 1 Tb. unsweetened cocoa powder. I like chopped walnuts best with this flavor combination.
MIDDLE LAYER: Substitute chocolate syrups and shake powders.
TOPPING: No change.
48 servings, each: 128 cal, 12 g fat (5 g sat.), 2 g carb, 5 g protein

EXPERIMENT WITH OTHER FLAVORS AND COMBINATIONS ~

You are limited only by your imagination and your supply of syrups, extracts, nuts, and nut butters!

Pancakes

- **2/3 cup** TLC Bake Mix (180 ml)
- **1 Tb. heavy cream** (15 ml)
- **1 Tb. oil** (15 ml)
- **1 Tb. SF vanilla flavor syrup** (15 ml)
- **1 egg**
- **2/3 cup water** (180 ml)

Whisk together gently and fry on a very hot greased griddle, turning once.

2 servings, each: **ULC:** *291 cal, 20 g fat (3 g sat.), 9 g carb (2 g fiber), 19 g protein* **MC***: 249 cal, 14 g fat (3 g sat.), 13 g carb (3 g fiber), 16 g protein* **SF:** *296 cal, 21 g fat (3 g sat.), 11 g carb (2 g fiber), 17 g protein*

Crepes

Simply add an additional 1/4 cup of water (60 ml) **and an additional egg to pancake batter.**

When cooking, ladle out small amounts and tilt the surface of pan so the thin batter will run over and cover the entire surface of pan, making very large thin pancakes that are suitable for wraps.

8 servings, each: **ULC:** *82 cal, 6 g fat (1 g sat.), 2 g carb ,5 g protein* **MC***: 72 cal, 4 g fat (1 g sat.), 3 g carb,4 g protein* **SF:** *83 cal, 6 g fat (0 g sat.), 2 g carb, 5 g protein*

Did you know ...

Use a meat baster to "squeeze" your pancake batter onto the hot griddle and you'll get perfectly shaped pancakes every time.

Peanut Butter Cookies

- **½ cup softened unsalted butter** (120 ml)
- **1 cup unsweetened peanut butter** (240 ml)
- **2 Tb. SF vanilla flavor syrup** (30 ml)
- **2 cups Splenda™ Granular** (480 ml)
- **2 eggs**
- **1 cup** TLC Bake Mix (240 ml)
- **¼ cup ground flax seed** (60 ml, or wheat bran)
- **4 Tb.** TLC Jelly or Jam (60 ml)

Preheat oven to 350 degrees F (180 C). Cream butter, peanut butter, vanilla syrup, and Splenda™ together, scraping bowl often. Beat in eggs. Stir flax meal or wheat bran into bake mix, then gradually add the dry ingredients to the wet ingredients already in the bowl, scraping sides of bowl and beaters at least once more. Using a standard 1/8 cup measure (to assure a uniform size), scoop out level measures of dough and roll into 24 round balls. Using your thumb, press down and make an indentation in the middle of each ball. Don't go too deep, or your cookies will fall apart - about halfway is perfect. Space cookies 1" apart on ungreased cookie sheets. Place a level ½ teaspoon of low carb jelly in each indentation. Bake approximately 15 minutes, or until cookies are lightly browned.
Allow to cool on cookie sheet for two to three minutes, then carefully remove to cooling racks.

8 servings, each: **ULC or SF:** *141 cal, 11 g fat (3 g sat.), 5 g carb,(1 g fiber), 5 g protein* **MC:** *136 cal, 10 g fat (3 g sat.), 6 g carb (1 g fiber), 4 g protein*

You can skip the jelly and just make the traditional crisscross marks with a fork, if you prefer regular peanut butter cookies. Or for an extra treat, fill the indentations with a square of low carb chocolate!

Peanut Butter Cupcakes

- **½ cup peanut butter** (120 ml)
- **3 Tb. softened unsalted butter** (45 ml)
- **¾ cup Splenda™ Granular** (180 ml)
- **1 Tb. molasses** (15 ml)
- **1 egg**
- **1 Tb. SF vanilla flavor syrup** (15 ml)
- **½ cup heavy cream** (120 ml)
- **¼ cup water** (60 ml)
- **1 cup** *TLC Bake Mix* (240 ml)

Preheat oven to 350 degrees F (180 C). Grease muffin tins well or line with paper liners. Cream peanut butter, butter and Splenda™ together. Add egg, syrup, cream, water, and molasses. Add bake mix and mix gently. Divide evenly between 12 muffin tins and bake until a toothpick inserted in the center comes out clean and the tops spring back when touched lightly, about 17-22 minutes.

12 servings, each: **ULC or SF:** *160 cal, 12 g fat (4 g sat.), 6 g carb,(1 g fiber), 6 g protein* **MC:** *149 cal, 11 g fat (4 g sat.), 7 g carb (1 g fiber), 5 g protein*

These would be delicious frosted with a mixture of ¼ cup (60 ml) **unsweetened peanut butter, ½ cup** (120 ml) **cream cheese and 2 Tb.** (30 ml) **sugar free syrup - I highly recommend French vanilla.**

Frosted, each: **ULC or SF:** *220 cal, 17 g fat (6 g sat.), 7 g carb,(1 g fiber), 8 g protein* **MC:** *207 cal, 16 g fat (6 g sat.), 8 g carb (1 g fiber), 7 g protein*

Pecan Pie

CRUST - I recommend, and included in my analysis, the all-purpose crust found on page 97.

PIE FILLING
- **3 eggs**
- **1 cup SF maltitol syrup** (240 ml)
- **1 tsp. vanilla extract** (5 ml)
- **1-2 tsp. caramel or butter rum flavoring** (5-10 ml)*
- **½ cup Splenda™ Granular** (120 ml)
- **3 Tb. melted butter** (45 ml)
- **1½ cups pecan halves** (360 ml)

Beat eggs until smooth; add syrup slowly, beating constantly; then add extracts, Splenda, and melted butter, in turn. *Depending on brand used and its concentration, you may need to adjust the extract measurement.

Arrange pecans in crust, then pour liquid ingredients over top. Bake at 425 degrees F (220 C) for 15 minutes. Reduce heat to 350 degrees F (180 C) and continue baking for about 15 more minutes.

12 decadent servings, each: 350 cal, 27 g fat (2 g sat.), 25 g carb (3 g fiber, 16 g sugar alcohols), 8 g protein.

Did you know ...

Store a little loose baking soda inside dry thermoses that you don't use very often and they will always be fresh when you do.

Peppermint Drops

- **8 oz. cream cheese** (225 gm)
- **1 cup Splenda™ Granular** (240 ml)
- **1½ cups vanilla protein powder** (360 ml)
- **½ tsp. peppermint extract** (2.5 ml)
- **¾ tsp. mint extract** (3.75 ml)
- **8 tsp. heavy cream, divided** (40 ml)
- **½ tsp. vanilla extract** (2.5 ml)
- **1 Tb. melted butter** (15 ml)
- **1 Tb. unsweetened cocoa powder** (15 ml)

Cream softened cream cheese with Splenda™, protein powder, 4 tsp. cream, and mint extracts. Drop by teaspoonfuls onto lightly oiled baking sheet and place in the freezer to chill. Batter should be loose enough to settle into round shapes easily. If it is not, add additional cream a few drops at a time until of the proper consistency.

Combine melted butter with 4 tsp. cream, vanilla, and cocoa powder. Drizzle over thoroughly chilled mint drops. Place into a sealed container and keep in freezer (sticky when not frozen).

Peppermint patty fans will be pleased! If you like a strong mint flavor, increase extracts to taste.

18 servings, each: 58 cal, 4 g fat (2 g sat.), 1 g carb, 3 g protein.

Vanilla Nut Muffins

- **2 cups vanilla protein powder** (480 ml)
- **½ cup Splenda™ Granular** (120 ml)
- **1 Tb. baking powder*** (15 ml)
- **2 Tb. SF vanilla syrup** (30 ml - could also use other flavors with a different flavor extract)
- **½ cup heavy cream** (120 ml)
- **½ cup sour cream** (120 ml)
- **1 Tb. vanilla extract** (15 ml)
- **3 eggs**
- **¼ cup water** (60 ml)
- **¼ cup oil** (60 ml)
- **½ cup chopped nuts** (120 ml - optional, could use berries)

Heat oven to 350 degrees F (180C) and line or oil 18 muffin tins. Stur together protein powder, Splenda™, and baking powder. Set aside. Beat eggs with water, oil, cream, vanilla extract, syrup, and sour cream. Combine with dry ingredients and stir just till moistened. Fold in nuts. Divide between tins and bake for 10-14 minutes, or until muffins test 'done' in the center.

*HIGH ALTITUDE: *Reduce baking powder to 2 tsp.*

18 servings, each: 119 cal, 8 g fat (3 g sat.), 2 g carb, 8 g protein

You could substitute *TLC Bake Mix* **for the protein powder and baking powder - in that case:**
ULC: *150 cal, 11 g fat (2 g sat.), 4 g carb,(1 g fiber), 8 g protein* **MC:** *132 cal, 9 g fat (2 g sat.), 6 g carb (1 g fiber), 6 g protein* **SF:** *152 cal, 11 g fat (2 g sat.), 5 g carb,(1 g fiber), 7 g protein*

TRIFLE: slice muffins in five pieces and layer with a complementary flavored serving of mousse (pg. 117) in a parfait, dessert, or wine glass.

Waffles

- **2/3 cup** *TLC Bake Mix* (180 ml)
- **1 Tb. heavy cream** (15 ml)
- **3 Tb. oil** (45 ml)
- **2 Tb. SF vanilla flavor syrup** (30 ml)
- **2 eggs**
- **½ cup water** (120 ml)

Separate eggs. Whip egg whites until stiff, and set aside. Whisk remaining ingredients together until well mixed. Fold in egg whites gently. Cook on hot waffle iron according to manufacturer's recommendations.

2 servings, each: **ULC:** *452 cal, 37 g fat (5 g sat.), 9 g carb, (2 g fiber), 23 g protein* **MC:** *410 cal, 31 g fat (5 g sat.), 14 g carb (2 g fiber), 19 g protein* **SF:** *457 cal, 38 g fat (4 g sat.), 11 g carb,(2 g fiber), 20 g protein*

Did you know ...

fabric softener sheets (even used ones) like the ones you use in the dryer will ...
- ✓ **Eliminate static electricity from your television screen? Wipe your television screen with a used fabric softener sheet to keep dust from resettling.**
- ✓ **Dissolve soap scum from shower doors?**
- ✓ **Eliminate static cling from pantyhose? Rub a damp, used sheet of fabric softener sheet over the hose.**
- ✓ **Collect pet hair? Rubbing an area with a fabric softener sheet will magnetically attract all the loose hairs.**

Zucchini Bran Muffins

- **1½ cups** *TLC Bake Mix* (360 ml)
- **3 eggs, separated**
- **¾ cup wheat bran** (180 ml)
- **½ cup oat bran** (120 ml)
- **½ cup Splenda™ Granular** (120 ml)
- **½ cup water** (120 ml)
- **1 tsp. ground cinnamon** (5 ml)
- **½ tsp. ground nutmeg** (2.5 ml)
- **¼ tsp. ground ginger** (1.25 ml)
- **½ cup SF vanilla flavor syrup** (120 ml)
- **1½ cups grated unpeeled zucchini** (360 ml – 7 oz. - 200 gm)

Preheat oven to 350 degrees F (180 C). Grease muffin tins well. Separate eggs. Whip egg whites until just stiff and set aside. Beat egg yolks until thick and lemon colored. Add Splenda™ and spices and mix well, scraping down beaters and sides of bowl at least once. Add grated zucchini, water, and SF syrup. Mix. Add bake mix and mix gently. Fold in egg whites. Divide between 12 muffin tins and bake until a toothpick inserted in the center comes out clean and the tops spring back when touched lightly – about 20-25 minutes.

12 servings, each: **ULC:** *162 cal, 11 g fat (0 g sat.), 10 g carb, (3 g fiber), 9 g protein* **MC:** *126 cal, 9 g fat (0 g sat.), 12 g carb (3 g fiber), 8 g protein* **SF:** *164 cal, 11 g fat (0 g sat.), 11 g carb,(3 g fiber), 8 g protein*

For an extra treat, top with streusel topping before baking: Melt 1 Tb. (15 ml) butter, add ½ cup Splenda™ Granular (120 ml) , 1 tsp. (5 ml) cinnamon, and ½ cup (120 ml) chopped walnuts. Sprinkle over muffin batter.

Adds, per muffin: 39 cal, 3 g fat, 1 g carb, 1 g protein

The following blank pages are provided as a handy place to insert notes, a carb counter, additional recipes, etc.

Spice It Up!

The difference between a really great cook, and a simply adequate cook, is often times due to the way they use (or don't use) spices. Walk into any commercial kitchen and watch a chef at work and one thing you'll notice real fast is that absolutely everything gets "seasoned", and usually more than once. The same holds true in my kitchen, where I wouldn't dream of cooking meat without adding additional flavors, in addition to salt and pepper. When meat is the centerpiece of a meal, it should be a memorable taste sensation, and never be bland or boring. A great way for busy cooks to save themselves some valuable time is by combining spices into an all-purpose dry rub for meat.

This recipe is listed in "parts" so you can make as much or as little as you want. If you use 1/8 cup per part, your yield will conveniently just fill a typical American "bulk" sized spice container.

ALL-PURPOSE MEAT SEASONING
8 parts garlic powder
8 parts onion powder
4 parts black pepper (you may prefer less)
2 parts seasoned salt
2 parts dry parsley (optional - mostly for looks)
2 parts paprika
1 part ground cumin
1 part cayenne pepper (optional - for spice masochists)
              1 carb per tsp.

Apply liberally to the outside of meat (beef, pork, lamb, elk, venison, poultry, etc.), prior to cooking. I like to rub it into the meat by hand and then allow the meat to sit on the counter for thirty minutes to one hour before cooking. This will help the meat to cook a little faster, too. (Of course you shouldn't allow uncooked meat to sit out any longer than it takes for it to reach room temperature, and you should always refrigerate cooked meat promptly.)

For great steaks, prick with a fork, rub in the spice mix, then marinate in a mixture of equal amounts of red wine & olive oil <u>or</u> Worcestershire & Soy sauces. While grilling, sprinkle with more spice mix. This method works particularly well with game meats. The wine cooks off, but you can substitute red wine vinegar, if you wish, diluted half and half with plain water.

All Sugars
Thou art my Downfall
Never my Lips
to pass!
Thy Work is done
My waistline's run
From Earth
all the way to Heaven
Give me this day
my Meat and my Cheese
And lead me not
into Carbo Temptation
But deliver me
from Low Fat Fanatics!
Forgive me my Keto Breath
As I forgive Those
who doubt
my Way Of Eating
and speak against me
For Low Carb is the Way
And the Truth
Shall prevail
Forever.

— Karen Rysavy

ISBN 0-9714929-1-3

52500

9 780971 492912